Further praise for
Brian Klemmer

"This is an absolute must read for the person who wants to enjoy life more, have more, and contribute to others at a very high level. Brian Klemmer captures the often elusive essentials in being a master of the game called life."
Mark Victor Hansen — Best Selling co-author of *Chicken Soup for the Soul*

"We were so impressed with Brian's training that we offered it to everyone in our factory! The effects were visable and immediate. Many, many employees thanked us for this opportunity to improve their personal lives. This book provides unique insights into the culture necessary for success in any organization. It focuses on people and personal responsibility. I recommend this to anyone who wants to improve themselves or their organization. It is more than a must read. It is a must do!" **Mike Simmons — Vice President Finance and Planning, The Fulton Group of Companies**

"We have used Brian for customer service training, sales training and for a management retreat over the last two years. This effort has helped us turn concepts like "partnership and teamwork" from words into action. This book now makes these principles available to everyone for producing results in their personal and professional life." **Jim MacDonald, President and CEO, R.F. MacDonald**

"This book is long overdue. Brian's training programs have been at the top of their class. The insights on fundamental life issues and personal communication as well as understanding the real meaning of commitment, self responsibility and relationships are what can make a business team excel or an individual achieve superior performance and happiness. This is truly one of the rare programs that have had a lasting and permanent impact on the participants and where positive improvements are measurable. Definitely an outstanding training experience. Many thanks to Brian as he has affected our lives in a most positive and memorable way." **Jim Kirkland – National Service Manager, American Suzuki Motor Company**

Quotes from high income earners in the network marketing industry

"Brian Klemmer is <u>*THE BEST*</u> *speaker I have heard. Now he has produced* <u>*THE BEST*</u> *book. I'm recommending that everyone in my downline read it."* **Tim Sales - Big Planet**

"The first chapter on the 3R's will significantly increase the quality of all your relationships as well as be a foundation for how to build your business relationships." **Dany and Debby Martin - NSA**

"The chapter on the Formula of Champions by itself is worth 1,000 times what someone will pay for this book. It is the single biggest insight to producing results I have seen." **Mitch Huhem – Rexall**

"Everyone wants to do well at their network marketing business. Many books tell you what to do. This book will take you from someone who merely works the business to be a business builder."
Jordan Adler – Excel Telecomunications

"If you are looking to make a dramatic increase in the effectiveness of your prospecting <u>*and*</u> *coaching of your downline, this is the book to read."* **Donna Larson Johnson – Arbonne**

"This book goes way beyond normal motivation and how to do the business and provides network marketers the missing keys to be tops in their business." **Jarman Massie – Royal Body Care**

"Brian Klemmer has keynoted at our convention and trained the key leaders in our team to success. Now he has captured the essence of his training in this book. It is a must read for anyone serious about their business." **Henry Brandt – Nature's Own**

Acknowledgements

This book is dedicated to my parents, Ken & Alice Klemmer who were everything a child could want in parents. My thanks to my wife Roma, and our 3 children Kelly, David, and Krystal who have been God's biggest blessing to me as well as some of my best teachers of the material in this book. Thanks to Mark Victor Hansen, best selling co-author of the *Chicken Soup for the Soul* series and John Gray, best selling author of *Men are From Mars and Women are From Venus*. Despite their mega-star status, they have continuously taken time to support me as well as believe in me over the years. Thanks to Lance Giroux of Allied Ronin for not only introducing me to this work, but being a great friend since 1968. Thanks to my mentor Tom who passed away in 1983 and was the vehicle for me learning most of this work. Thanks to Tony Giovanni for his technical support in making this book a reality and never once complaining about any of my changes or demands. Thanks to all of our clients who have believed in K&A and the many thousands of participants who through their willingness to explore ways to be more successful and contribute to others have given me hope. Thanks lastly to all the people who have made K&A a career and dedicated their lives to "A World that Works for Everyone with no one left out".

If how-to's were enough

We would all be skinny, rich and happy!

Brian Klemmer

Table of Contents

Prelude

Welcome to the journey of personal growth called Personal Mastery. It is a journey that begins each day, but never ends. It is an exciting exploration of how you play the game of life and how your choices create your results. It is a journey available to all…and yet chosen by few.

Today you got up, went through your morning rituals and embarked on the tasks of the day. Whether your mission involved leading a company or caring for a small child, you were called to make thousands of choices over the course of the day. Which of these choices are costing you the results you truly wish for? The path of Personal Mastery enables you to discover both what is behind those choices that don't support you and what you really want. It enables you to make different choices.

As you might imagine, the path is not always easy. It takes courage and commitment. You have to care a great deal about your results to work through the discomfort that characterizes breakthrough personal growth. Yet the rewards are incredible. Life is more fulfilling, less stressful, more fun. You are able to achieve your goals and to invent or create new ones.

Sound exciting? It is.

The intent of this book is to assist you in becoming a master of the game of life, able to create success as you define it and on your own terms. I feel blessed and honored for the opportunity to share with you what I have learned, with the help of many who went before me, along the path of Personal Mastery.

I applaud your willingness to be open, to have the courage to explore, and to re-examine some of your fundamental beliefs about life—who you are, what you think life is, what success is, and what you believe it requires to be successful. To best take advantage of this book I have included suggestions you may choose to follow:

- **Take time with this book,** to digest and continually re-explore its meaning for you. When a book is savored, not gulped is when the fullest appreciation is achieved. Your success will be measured, not in how quickly you finish it, but in how much your viewpoint or perspective is changed.

- **Write in it.** When you relate your own personal experience in life to a line or story on these pages, write it in. During your first time reading, highlight actions that have special meaning in one color. The next time you read the book, highlight what jumps out in a different color. This will allow you to add emotion and speed the process of change.

- **Be consistent.** A garden is best watered a little bit at a time on a consistent basis rather than flooding it all at once. Set up a plan of daily reading for a month and then follow it.

• **Allow yourself to react.** It will not serve you to agree with what is written or to disagree. It will be in the struggle to gain different perspectives or viewpoints that your thinking will shift. It is the premise of this book that "To Think Is To Create." If this is true and you want to create new results in your life—a better marriage—more income—a closer relationship to God—more self-confidence—whatever it is—then that new result will absolutely require new thinking or a different perspective. The results in your life will be the measure of the depth of your understanding that sentence. My mentor taught me "There is no fairer way to gauge anything than by results - often harsh, but always fair." Allow this book to assist you in deepening your understanding of "To Think Is To Create."

• **Apply it.** Involve yourself in life. As you will discover, "To Think Is To Create" is not a "head-trip," but an active process. As you begin to live applying your new thinking, you will get feedback from life. Re-read the book apply a new changed perspective until those results and goals that you truly want are achieved.

"99% of all your decisions you do not make — your programs make them for you and you think you are choosing"

Chapter One
The Secret

The Question: Is success that complicated or have you just missed something?

Most people in their search to "be better" look for some "how- to's" or techniques or skills. They want to be wealthy so they look for someone to teach them "how- to". They want a better marriage so they look for a "how -to". They want to lose weight so they look for a "how-to". They want a better relationship with their creator so they look for a "how-to". They want to be better at sports, sales, parenting - you name it - and they want the "how-to". The problem is - it doesn't work. If "how-to's" were enough, a top sales person would simply teach others how to sell and everyone would be a good sales person . A good student would teach study skills and everyone would be a good student. A great manager would teach all executives how to manage and the executives would all be great managers. If "how-to's" were enough we would all be skinny, rich, and happy.

The truth of the matter is most people do not do what they are told, nor do they do what they know is good for themselves. People behave according to their fundamental beliefs or their subconscious thinking. Another way to say this is that 99% of all the decisions you think you are making, you don't make. Your subconscious, or belief system, is what is making your decisions and yet all along you thought you were the one doing the deciding. This astounding fact is the secert of the ages.

For example, If you want more liberty in your life then you must examine your beliefs and how they are affecting your life. I will define Liberty as the ability to go where you want, when you want to go, not when someone else says you can or can't. It is the ability to have what you want to have when you want to have it, not when your pocketbook or bank balance says you can or can't. It is the ability to do what you want to do when you want to do it. Most importantly, it is the ability to be what you want to be when you want to be it. Liberty is the result of wise decisions made for us by our subconscious. Freedom is the ability to decide and liberty is the result of wise decisions.

If it is true that 99% of all our decisions are made for us, or even that a majority are made by our subconscious, then we are not deciding and liberty is about as likely as winning the lottery.

What kind of decisions are we talking about? All decisions. Decisions about how you communicate, or don't communicate with your children. Decisions about how to try and sell something or even whether you like sales. Decisions about whether to buy this book or not. Decisions like how you feel right now. Decisions like whether you have a job, own a business or are an investor. Decisions of whether you show up on time or are late. All kinds of decisions.

Some of these decisions are conscious and by that I mean that you are aware of the choice. Most decisions though are made without your awareness. These are the ones you want to explore in order to have more liberty and create the life you say you want.

Imagine I was born with a pair of dark green sunglasses on. A pretty ridiculous sight I agree. Let's now say I have had them on my whole life and I look at the paper these words are on. I would say it's green. If you tried to tell me it was white, I would tell you that you were wrong, that you didn't know what you were talking about, even that you better go get your eyes checked. It wouldn't matter to me how excited or persistent you were, because I couldn't see white even if I truly wanted to. There would be no hope or possibility of my seeing white.

If I learned there was something called sunglasses and I started looking for sunglasses, I might discover I had them on. If I took them off, in a matter of seconds, I would be able to see what I literally could not see just seconds before, the white page. It is often like this in our lives when someone tells us that we can make more money or get a job done in half the time or work a problem out in a relationship. Even though we want the result, we can't see it as possible. Robert Kiyosaki, author of the best-selling, *Rich Dad, Poor Dad*, tells people they can be multi-millionaires. He knows they can. He went from being homeless, to being a millionaire in less than 5 years. However, most people listening to him just can't see it as real for themselves. Peggy Long is an extremely successful individual in a network marketing company, a good friend and a client. She will look at someone and know that they have what it takes to be financially independent, but they can't see it, even though they want it.

The key is to look for the sunglasses that are screening you from seeing the solutions you want. This is why you cannot teach success. A person must experientially (not intellectually) begin to "see" things, life, themselves differently. This is in essence what we assist individuals in doing in our Personal Mastery workshops whether it be during a corporate or a public seminar.

Let's look at this principle another way. Imagine you live in Kansas City and you hire me to speak with your company. You send me a map and instructions on how to get to your office. There is only one problem. Unknown to you, the printer made a mistake. The map you sent was really of Minneapolis even though it said Kansas City at the top. When I get to the airport and to my rental car and try to find your place, what happens? I get lost, frustrated and confused. (The way many people feel as they try and get ahead in life.) None of the names on the map match your instructions and I can't find the right streets. I call you on my cellular phone and tell you that this isn't working.

Now, let's say you have a belief map of how the world works. Your map says that the way people get ahead is to work harder. You may know someone in your life who thinks like that. You would tell me that I just need to work harder. I'm coachable and say "OK." I now start driving twice as fast—I am working harder. What happens now? I get a ticket. I'm still lost and very frustrated. I call you again and read you the riot act.

Let's say you have another map of the way the world works that says "attitude is the key". Have you ever heard that? The height of your altitude depends on your attitude. You would tell me, "Brian, I can tell the problem. You have a bad attitude." "You are darn right I have a bad attitude." I'd reply. You would calm me down and tell me to go read a positive thinking book. I'm coachable and I've done Evelyn Wood's speed-reading so I read a positive thinking book. When I start driving, what happens? I'm still lost, only now I don't care, because I have a positive attitude!

In terms of solving the problem—getting to your office—I still haven't made it. The problem is the map, not my attitude or how hard I worked. I simply have the wrong map for Kanas City. What if you have the wrong map of who you are? Or what commitment is? Or what responsibility is? You could work real hard, have a great positive attitude and still not create your dreams.

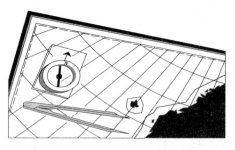

Many of you honestly believe you have the right maps. But do you really? If you are not getting the results you want, then in that area, you don't have the right map. This does not mean that there is anything wrong with you. In fact, there isn't anything wrong with you. God doesn't make any mistakes. You just have the wrong map.

Let's assume you had great parents like I did. You then have a map of good parenting. It's not a theory. You have experienced good parenting. The only problem is the world has changed. When I was a teenager, my biggest decision was which girl to kiss. At the time of writing this book, I have two teenage sons and a 12 year old daughter. My two teenage sons biggest decision is, do I accept a line of cocaine at a party—not which girl to kiss (well maybe that too!). The world has changed and so the map that worked for my parents will not work for my children and me. When I was a child, it worked to not talk openly about sex at too early an age. The world has changed with diseases such as AIDS that make that old map no longer effective.

This is also why it doesn't work to simply copy someone who is successful. Yes, modeling or copying someone who is successful is a "how to", but maybe you are different from that person or in a different situation, and it requires a different map. This is why two individuals in a seminar of ours make entirely different discoveries even though they did the same exercise. They each discover the different sunglasses or maps they have.

One of the most exciting parts about all of this is how long it takes to take a set of sunglasses off. Seconds. Major advancements in your life can occur quickly. It does not have to take a long time. I have seen thousands of what appear to be miracles occur in incomes, relationships, and health as a result of just a weekend of work. A weekend of finding sunglasses and taking them off.

One of the most important maps - and it really involves several maps, is "Who are you?" What you think you are often times is more important than who you really are. A beginning step in exploring this question, is the following model of what we have just been discussing.

Think of an M&M's candy with a nut in the middle. The color coating on the outside is your behavior. The white candy that comes next is your feelings. The chocolate is then your thinking, your subconscious thinking or programs. The inner most part is the nut—you!

There is a lot to this simple model of you. First, are you how you behave? I would say you are not. Some people get programmed or believe at a deep level that they are their behavior, their job, their results. For example, let's say a parent catches a child stealing a candy bar and says, "You are a bad boy or girl". The child could, although not necessarily, then begin to believe that "Oh, I did something bad and they say I am bad. I am my behavior." The problem with this set of sunglasses is that your self esteem goes on a yo yo ride. When you behave well it goes up and when you behave bad or get poor results it goes down. If you understand that your behavior is much like your jacket—it's not you—you just wear it and it has nothing to do with who you are, you can have high self esteem no matter what the circumstances.

Are you your feelings? Again, I would suggest that you are not your feelings. If your behavior is your jacket, then your feelings are your shirt or blouse. Much like the M&M, they touch each other and affect each other. Suppose Sally and Mary love to dance. They usually go dancing every Friday night. Sally has had a bad day at work and Mary calls her up and asks her to go dancing. Sally might say, "No, I don't feel like it." Her bad feelings just determined her behavior. Let's say Mary insists and together they go dancing for a couple hours, even though initially Sally didn't "feel" like dancing. Now how does Sally feel? Better! She changed how she behaved and in return changed how she felt. If you are ever not feeling the way you want to feel or hear someone say "you need to change your attitude," you know what to do. Change your behavior. Go for a walk, sing a song, jump up and down. Do something different. However, there is a problem. The changed feeling won't last. This is often why positive-pep-rally -type motivational seminars don't work in terms of sustaining change. What truly determines your behavior and how you feel is your subconscious thinking 99% of the time. **To change from the outside in is easy, but it is short lived.** This does not mean change from the outside in isn't important. Sometimes you need a "quick fix". If you have just had an argument at home and you are on your way to an important sales or management meeting, you can use a short-term fix. Try jumping up and down and yelling, "I'm excited!" It may seem foolish, but you will feel better and you will make better decisions, more sales or just be more effective. Just know that it won't last.

For long term change, look for your sunglasses, your maps or subconscious beliefs. Once you see white, you can never go back to not knowing that white exists. It is a revelation. I have a plaque a friend gave me years ago. It appears as just a bunch of match sticks on a board. My friends laughed, "Don't you see it?" I struggled and got frustrated because it looked like a bunch of matchsticks. Then they told me the sticks spelled JESUS if you looked at it properly, with different sunglasses. Sure enough, I saw it. Now when I look at the plaque, I can not help but see that it spells Jesus. It is exactly the same way as when we see through from different sunglasses. Once you have pierced the veil of the sunglasses, you will begin to see things differently.

"On this rock I stand and the whole world can adjust to me."

WILLIAM PENN PATRICK

Chapter Two **RESULTS**
The Formula of Champions

The Question: Are you getting something other than what you want?

Once upon a time there was a young boy named Aladdin. As he was kicking up the sand on a beach, he stubbed his toe on an old lamp. It looked intriguing so he took it home. He spent hours chipping away the clods of sand and then got his toothbrush out and began to really clean it. All of a sudden a genie appeared and said to him, "Your wish is my command!" Aladdin was obviously stunned and he decided to test the genie. He asked for a Big Mac hamburger. Puff! He got a Big Mac. Stunned, he then asked for something bigger, a camel. Puff! A camel appeared. He began to get really excited. He soon asked for all the normal material things such as a house, clothes, money. Then Aladdin left his lamp on the shelf and went on a cruise around the world.

While he was gone, one of the maid servants wanting to impress Aladdin and gain his favor, decided to do some house cleaning and picked up Aladdin's room. A merchant in the streets below was yelling out, "Lamps for sale! Lamps for sale!" Not knowing the value of the magic lamp, the maid decided to trade the old lamp for a newer looking one. When Aladdin finally returned from the cruise many months later, he went looking for the lamp. When he couldn't find it, he began to panic. He called in his servants and asked if anyone had seen the old lamp. The maid proudly stated what she had done. Aladdin fell to his knees and wailed uncontrollably. He then vowed that he would spend the rest of his life looking for that lamp and that when he found it, he would never again let it out of his sight.

Aladdin spent the next ten years looking for the lamp. When at long last he discovered the shop with his magic lamp, he was destitute and without money. Not being able to afford the lamp he offered to work for one year to buy the lamp. The new owner, not knowing the lamp's value, agreed. At the end of that year of sweeping floors, closing up shop and doing whatever the shop owner requested, Aladdin was the owner of the lamp. The lamp never again left his sight and was always protected at great expense.

There are many great lessons in this story. The formula of champions I am about to share with you is just like Aladdin's lamp.

Are you willing to spend a year, tremendous energy, and perhaps thousands of dollars to really learn and understand this formula? It took Aladdin time and energy to first clean the lamp and then later to earn the lamp when he did not have any money. There is no free lunch in life. You will have to work to understand and be able to apply this formula to produce results. If you do understand and apply it, the formula, it will literally produce millions of dollars for you and many quality relationships as well as whatever else your heart desires. What if I gave you a magic lamp? Suppose this formula that I am talking about could produce for you anything that you wanted. You would be excited, wouldn't you? I am about to give you the most powerful formula I know. It has been used by Olympic athletes, Fortune 500 company executives, best selling authors, world renown scientists, and master musicians to name a few. The challenge for you will be in understanding the formula.

The formula of champions has long proven itself against the acid test of time, but you must spend time experiencing it in order to understand its full value. I personally would not take any amount of money to forget this formula. I have used it to raise millions of dollars for a cause I believed in, even though I had no experience in raising that amount of money. I used it to bring into my life my beautiful wife and to create our long-lasting, fulfilling relationship. I was 34 years old, single, never married, and believed it wasn't possible. I have used the formula to buy houses with no money. I say these things not to brag, but to give you hope. I am just like you. If you had a recipe for great chocolate chip cookies, you wouldn't have to have a great personality, or a higher education to create great cookies. You simply need to follow the formula, the recipe. It is just so with this formula. Here it is:

INTENTION + MECHANISM = RESULT

If you are anything like I was, you are saying to yourself "so what?" That doesn't seem so special. This is because at this moment it is only information in your conscious mind. You must make the formula part of your heart (Proverbs 23:7) or subconscious for it to have the power of Aladdin's lamp. You must apply this and wrestle with it on a daily basis. Digest it. Let's begin that process by defining the pieces of the formula:

INTENTION. According to the dictionary: "1: a determination to act in a certain way 2: purpose, aim, end". It is not merely willpower. Willpower comes from the conscious mind. Intention is a knowingness which comes from a deeper level (covered in Chapter 5.) It is a deep clarity with intensity. It is focus, certainty, commitment. It is many things.

MECHANISM. According to the dictionary: "1: a piece of machinery; also: a process or technique for achieving a result." A mechanism is then simply a vehicle or way to accomplish something —it is the "how- to."

RESULTS. According to the dictionary: "1: something that happens: effect, consequence". A result is what you have after combining an intention and a mechanism.

What if your intention always equaled your result? I am going to suggest that is the way that it already is. Your intention always equals your result.

Before you argue too hard—look at your hand. Let's call the front of your hand the palm and the other side, the back of your hand. Suppose you asked me for the front of my hand. Being the committed and giving guy I am, I take out a knife and slice off the front of my hand. But, what do I still have?

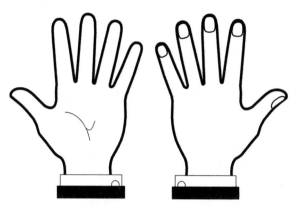

I still have a front and a back of my hand. You persist. You feel you are not communicating very well today and tell me you don't like backs and you only want the front of my hand. I take my knife and slice off another piece. What do I still have? A front and a back. Can I have a front without a back? No. They are inseparable. You can tell them apart, but they are inseparable. They do a dance together. Where one is, so is the other. The front of your hand is intention, the back of your hand is result.

This formula can be used retroactively to look at the past and see what your "real" intentions were. It can also be used proactively toward the future to create the results you want.

Let's imagine you had set a goal of making $100,000 in a year and you only achieved $70,000. Using the formula and examing your result means $100,000 was not your real intention. This is not to say you didn't want $100,000. You did. But your want was more like an idle wish. It was not your deepest, most focused commitment. Perhaps your intention was not to look foolish and so in working towards earning the $100,000, you were sure not to do anything that would make you look foolish. You fulfilled that deeper, more focused desire instead of making the $100,000. Perhaps you were unwilling to do something which might have appeared ridiculous or might have been interpreted as "pushy". It resulted in a lost sale and the opportunity to make the $100,000.

Imagine being on one side of a room and I told you to go back and forth across the room 100 times. Now imagine that each time you cross the room you must use a different mechanism. Perhaps you walk across and then crawl back. That's two mechanisms. Then you swim across and can't think of a way back. The swimming, crawling, and walking were all "mechanisms".

What is your intention? Some would say it is to keep crossing the room. How would you know that? Simply because I told you to? I suggest you cannot tell a person's true intention by what someone else tells them to do. When you tell your children to study, it does not necessarily mean that it is their intention to study. Corporations hire Klemmer & Associates all the time because they have told employees what to do, in the form of quotas, yet the people are not accomplishing the quotas. They are going through the motions, but are not totally committed to the goal. The results fall short of the goal. Reaching the quotas was not their intention. I am going to suggest you cannot even tell what a person's intention is by what they tell you they are committed to. In the K&A Personal Mastery seminars, we have people who tell us it is their intention to be financially independent. The truth of the matter is that it is not their intention to be financially independent. We know this because they are not taking risks in any way. They want to be wealthy. They have a wish to be wealthy. But that is very different than what we are referring to as true intention. We have people who say their intention is to have a happy marriage and yet "they are constantly trying to prove which of them is wrong." It is their true intention to be right- not to be happy. They definitely want a happy marriage, but it is not their true intention.

In this formula, we are not using intention the way the person who said "the road to hell is paved with good intentions" defined intention. That is simply a wish or a want. The true intention is much deeper, stronger, focused. A person's true intention is often hidden from himself or herself. I am suggesting the only way you can tell a person's true intention is by the results they have. I am suggesting that intention and result are always one and the same. You cannot have an intention without a corresponding result. Did you set New Year's resolutions last year and not reach them? Then this formula is saying it was not your "true" intention to keep those resolutions. Your true, deeper, driving intention was to something else. Perhaps it was to be comfortable, or right about why something couldn't be done, or to look good to your peers.

When I do this exercise of crossing the room in live seminars or at large conventions, I will wait until someone gets stuck. They can't think of another mechanism. People will cheer them on and at some point an idea comes to them seemingly out of the blue. It is not out of the blue. A scientifically proven process has taken place. **When the intent is clear and intense, a mechanism will always appear.** In essence, a voice inside their head (actually their subconscious) said something like, "I am not going to stand here like a fool. Come up with a mechanism and come up with it NOW!" And the subconscious responds with an idea for a new mechanism. This is a multi-million dollar concept. You do **not** have to know what to do - the mechanism. You **do** have to have an incredibly intense and clear intent. The intention always comes before the mechanism and true intention and commitment will always create the mechanism.

Everyone is familiar with John F. Kennedy's declaration that the U.S. was going to put a man on the moon by the end of the 1960's. Most people thought it was impossible because the science to do so, the mechanism, did not even exist. Yet Kennedy's intention created the science or mechanism. Business examples of this process are also abundant.

Most people, however, are wearing sunglasses that are mechanism-oriented. They do not want to even commit to goals until they have the "how-to" or mechanism in mind. They do not even start unless they have the mechanism in mind. They have it backwards. To further get themselves in a hole, most people wear a set of sunglasses that limits the number of mechanisms to accomplish one thing. They want to buy a house and they think there are only one or two ways. I can borrow 80% and put 20% down. When this mechanism doesn't work, their solution is to give up on the goal. Maybe they will try a second method, and if that doesn't work, they will surely give up. This is why I have people cross the room many times and wait when they get stuck until they discover another way across.

The real key to the formula is to raise your intention so high that you **have** to get the goal. Raise it so high you **must** get across the room. Your highest intention will always win. There must be no alternative but to get across the room. Every business owner I have ever met said "Yes, that is how I want my people to act." There are several ways to raise your intention to be more intense than those intentions you already have that are counter to the results you want.

• **Committing out loud to a friend that believes in you is one way to increase your intention.** Have you ever noticed that if you agree to excercise with friends you are more likely to do so? You have simply put to work your intention to not be embarrassed against your intention to be comfortable or lazy and not exercise.

• **Putting yourself at risk of gaining or losing money increases intention.** Imagine you wanted to buy a house in 90 days. Now imagine you wrote a check for $10,000 to a charity and said to a friend, "if I do not purchase a house in 90 days, cash the money and give it to a charity". Would your intention, desire, commitment to buy a house be higher? I suspect it would be.

- **Visualization increases intention.** This is why athletes, religious leaders and scientists all urge people to use some structured form of visualization. If you doubt this, look at a new car on a sales lot until a sales person arrives. They will often ask you, "Can you see yourself driving this automobile?" If you say, "No I can't," they will usually not even continue to talk to you. Because they know that if you were to apply to even one bank and they told you that you didn't qualify for a loan, that you would give up on your goal of buying a new car. On the other hand if you said, "I sure can see myself driving it, but I can't afford this car," they will usually respond with "get on in." After test driving it, your subconscious just has to have the car and it will change your tone of voice, your work ethic and who you talk to for prospects. It will cause you to change jobs and anything else it has to so that you can afford the new car. Your increased intention will produce a mechanism seemingly from nothing. Yet the average person won't even go looking for a new car until they have a way to afford it - the mechanism.

Learn how average people think. They are average because of how they think, not because of their education, or who they know, or where they were born, their age or any other external factor.

Next study how successful people think. **To think is to create.** If you do not know how successful people think, you will have difficulty reproducing their success. It is not their personality we are talking about in this formula. It is their subconscious thinking or fundamental beliefs about reality that is creating their result.

"Anger — is man or woman's last desperate attempt to avoid responsibility and blame the situation on someone or something else"

Chapter Three
The Key to Relationships

The Question: Who or what are you resisting? What price are you paying for this resistance?

Once upon a time, a small boy and girl were building a sand castle on the beach. They spent hours building towers, walls, and a moat. Slowly, while they were building the castle, the tide crept in closer. Finally, after working on this castle for most of the morning, a big wave came in and wiped it all away. An adult who was watching all of this was at first feeling sorry for the children because of all the work they had put into building the castle. Then the adult saw the children hold hands and run together laughing down the beach. It was then that the adult realized that although it is fun building empires, the lasting fun is in having friends with whom you can continue to laugh and be with long after all that you have spent your life building has washed away.

Relationships are the key to making almost anything happen. Relationships are the foundation to the quality of our life as well as the results we get. Take a look around you at anything man-made. Perhaps you see a salt and pepper shaker on your table. How many people do you suppose were involved in the shakers being on your table? There were people who ran machines in manufacturing them, as well as the packaging and labels they came in. Supervisors and secretaries who answered phones, sales people who sold it to the stores. There were investors for the company. Truck drivers who delivered it and on and on. Being "people smart " can make up for a lack of knowledge in many other areas. Can you begin to see the need to master relationships?

The key to relationships is often as simple as stopping one very common self-destructive thought process or program. It affects all your relationships both professionally and personally. By destructive, I mean this thought process costs money, ruins communication and destroys teamwork. It is the root behind all divorce and it costs businesses billions of dollars with no exaggeration. It causes loneliness and will even create physical illness in the body of the person who thinks this way. This way of thinking is like drinking poison.

Why are we even discussing such a negative thought process? Why not just discuss the positive? Because you think this way. Every human being I have ever met around the world, without exception, has experienced this self-destructive thought process. This way of thinking was probably formed by the age of six months old and now it is an ingrained part of most people's lives. The degree to which you master **not** getting caught in this thought process will translate to the the degree of quality in your relationships.

Why would intelligent people like you and I practice such a negative thought process? Perhaps it's because we don't connect this thought process directly to the damage it creates. If you touched a hot stove but the burn didn't show up for six months - you might touch it frequently because you didn't realize the connection. No one changes their way of being until they see the price they are paying is too high for what they are creating. Most of the time we don't tell the truth about the costs or prices because it hurts us to accept it. Open up to the true hurt this thought process causes you **and** others in your life and you will resolve to reduce or eliminate this thought process in your life.

The thought process I am speaking of is called "THE 3R'S"

RESENTMENT - RESISTANCE - REVENGE

- **RESENTMENT:** Any emotional reaction we view as negative to what we think was said or done
- **RESISTANCE:** The cutting off of communication or putting up a wall
- **REVENGE:** The attempt to get even or to settle the score.

What are some of our emotions which would fit the definition of resentment? Anger, frustration, sadness, jealousy, and hate are examples. These emotional reactions come from many different events in our lives. We can experience resentment when our spouse squeezes the toothpaste tube in the middle. Your child talks back to you or someone cuts you off on the highway. You are laid off when a company restructures. Someone you love dies. The examples are countless. If you are not experiencing resentments you are emotionally numb or dead, if not physically dead. Resentment is a natural part of life. Life is full of situations where we experience resentment. Forty thousand people starve to death everyday. How could you not be in resentment, unless you are emotionally numb? Even if you are numb, you are experiencing resentment and are likely just covering it up. It is probably still there, it still hurts. Most people live in a world of indifference for this very reason.

Some people are programmed that resentment is inherently bad. That is their set of sunglasses— that there is something wrong with experiencing resentment. Resentment is a fact of life. If you think it is bad, you can suppress the negative reactions and then get mad because you are mad! You are then in an endless cycle—a computer do-loop. Resentment will happen no matter how good the relationship you are in and no matter how good a company you work for. Resentment will happen as a part of being in the world. The real question is how will you handle it? Your thinking could create the day that turns your life around to the positive. It could also create the day that destroys you by moving into the 2nd R - RESISTANCE.

There are many ways we resist. A married couple gets in an argument (1st R) and then the husband rolls over to one side of the bed and the wife turns the other way. Their not talking to each other is resistance. Communication has been cut off and prices are being paid. Not talking is not the only way to resist. When a person is procrastinating or confused , they are in resistance to something. When a customer is being difficult and we slip behind the counter, the physical separation is the wall or resistance. We have a problem at home and we bury ourselves in our work or the television or sleep or food-that is resistance. When we insist on "being right" about our viewpoint—the lack of openness is resistence. I suggest making a list of the ways you resist. What do you resist?

Most often we are resisting in order to stay in or gain control. Here begins a fundamental problem in our belief systems or how we see reality. In the live seminar, I will ask a particpant to sit facing me in a chair. I then ask them to raise their arms and hands, palms facing me. I push on their hands. Almost always they push back and almost tip over backwards in the chair. Take note of TWO very important things. Number one—they pushed back. Why? Because they are not in control. Earlier in chapter one I stated that 99% of all our behavior we do not decide—our subconcious thinking decides for us. Our set of sunglasses makes the decision. In this case, most people have a program, a voice in their head, that says, "if someone pushes on you, you must push back to survive." The person on the chair instantly pushes back "to survive." The problem is that they don't survive. The chair tips causing them to fall backward and one of our people catches them. Think of a time when a child or boss or parent or lover or employee has pushed on you. Emotionally perhaps they tried to prove you wrong. Did you push back? Did you argue with them or perhaps try to make them wrong?

Now comes critical point number two. Your belief is false! You think it's necessary to push back to survive to not be taken advantage of and to gain or maintain control. Yet what happened in the chair demonstration? The person pushing back LOST CONTROL! They even fall over backward if they keep resisting. This clearly demonstrates when you resist, you lose control, not gain it. Why do our children make us mad? Because they get control! That's why they do it! After you have an argument with a child, how are they five minutes later? Fine. How are you five hours later? Steam still coming out your ears? Why? Because you are resisting reality. A little voice inside you is saying, "it shouldn't be this way", but it is. Resistance occurs when people say to themselves *it shouldn't be this way.*

What you resist—persists. Read that again. What you resist—persists. It prolongs what you don't want. So, what are you resisting? Perhaps it is your age? Or maybe it's your weight? That you are alone? Technology advancements that you do not understand? Who are you resisting? What about your job are you resisting? Perhaps making cold calls or paperwork or something monotonous? What price are you paying for your resistance? What prices are others or your company paying for your resistance? Remember, no one changes until they see the price they and others are paying is higher than they want to pay for what they are creating.

I am not recommending you become a door mat by not resisting, or even to let yourself be taken advantage of. Nor am I saying to be passive. That doesn't work. How can you not resist and also not let yourself be taken advantage of at the same time? One of the best analogies is for Marital Arts. In most Martial Arts what is taught is not to resist. Let the attacking force go by you and in fact use that very same force to lay them on the ground. In the classic movie, "The Karate Kid," the Master did not tell the teenager to let himself be bullied or abused. In AIKIDO, another martial art, you protect yourself and the attacker. There is no separation. We conduct sales seminars, using this metaphor to create top performers. Resist objections and you become a non-performer. Relate with objections as though they are your friend who is helping you to close the sale and you become a top performer.

One of my students, years ago, was a gentleman named Bob Tourtelot. He was then and is still a very successful attorney. He was very skeptical at first of this perspective. He had gained much of his success in law through intimidation in the courtroom. After the workshop, he called to relate his practical application of this concept. While in a multi-million dollar negotiation, another attorney yelled at him, trying to intimidate him. He said that previous to the workshops he would have yelled back (if not broke the other attorney's pointing finger)! He would have intellectually and emotionally tried to dominate the other attorney, but he remembered the 3R's were self-destructive. He said, "Thank you for having the courage to share your anger with me." One of the most incredible things in 20 years of negotiating occurred next. He gained control of the entire room instantly and everyone else knew it. It made him a lot of money. Bob was elated. How can you protect yourself without resisting? This brings us to the final R - Revenge. It is simply defined as a attempt to even the score. The key word in this definition is attempt. You can not get even. It's an impossibility. It violates God-given laws of this world. First, let's look at how people attempt to get even at work. In the business world, to get even, employees slow down, take a longer lunch break than authorized, call in sick when they are not, "borrow" company property (theft), participate in negative gossip — all in an attempt to get even for resentments they carry towards the business. How is it done in personal relationships? The silent treatment, denial of sex, running up the credit card, not doing our chores are common examples. It is repeated a thousand ways in an attempt to even the score.

The key to remember is: the **3R's are self-destructive.** When you resist or revenge, it hurts you. What you put out, you get back. What you sow is what you reap. The law on the street is what goes around, comes around. We have all heard it one way or another. How many children do you know who get mad at a parent and try to get even by getting bad grades or messed up on drugs? Classic 3R's. The child pays an incredible price. Thousands of ex-husbands and wives have done our workshops and start seeing how they have been using their own children to get even with the other parent and the child ends up paying a horrific price.

I have consulted with businesses, especially after downsizing, where the 3R's is rampant. People resist making tough decisions, market changes, friends being let go. They were headed toward putting the company out of business with their resistance. This really is a killer thought process. It is like the story of the pied piper which led the children to their deaths. If you follow the 3R tune you are headed for destruction. The sports world has in the past been rocked by major strikes. the strikes were driven by the 3R's. People resented others making more money than they felt was right.

When the 3R's is making your decisions, reason and logic no longer matter. People have religion shoved down their throats as a child and then later cut themselves off from God and have nothing to do with religion as their way to resist and to revenge. I consider this a huge price to pay. Look for how you are involved in the 3R's in your life. Where are you mad at yourself for something in your past? Where are you trying to get even? Silly isn't it? Tragic is more the word I'd use.

Is there ever any good reason for being in the 3R's? Suppose I threw a cup of water at you. Would you have a good reason to be in the 3R's? No! How about when a child is molested? Do they have a good reason to be in the 3R's? No! Why not? Because it is self-destructive. It hurts the person who thinks this way. I'm not saying you shouldn't get upset. You have a great reason to be upset. What I am saying is, if they allow it to go into resistance or revenge, they will pay a higher price than they want to pay. How would they pay? I don't know. We would have to ask them. Maybe the price is with physical illness, or unfulfilled relationships, living in the past and not being excited about the present or by denying God and falling from grace.

What then are some solutions if you are in the 3R's? There are many. Here are three key ones.

- **GIVING**
- **OPEN, HONEST, RESPONSIBLE COMMUNICATION**
- **FAIR FIGHTING**

These are often not solutions you feel like using. But why live your life by what you feel like doing rather than by letting what really matters to you make your choices? The solutions are not comfortable if you are in the 3R's because you want to get even. Giving when in resentment is an abnormal response given our programmed subconcious thinking.

Solution number one is giving. When you give something nice to a person you are in resentment with, does mean the person is going to be nice back? Not necessarily. This is not being manipulative to try and change the other person. You don't control them. So why then are you giving? You are giving in order to handle your own 3 R's. You don't want yourself or anyone you care for to pay any prices for being in resentment. Suppose someone in your office is inconsiderate to you. If you stay in resentment you will not be as creative at the office, you won't sell as well, you'll go home and your family might pay a price for you being in a poor mood.

The average person gives less when they are in resentment. *Learn to be a giving maniac.* Give when it is comfortable and when it is uncomfortable. Give when it looks like you will get back and give when it looks like you won't get back. Give when you know the recepient and give when you don't. Be a giving maniac not to be noble, but to be practical. All nobility is suspect. Give because there is a universal law that says what you put out, you will get back. What you sow so shall you reap. What goes around, comes around. However, the universal law does not say it will come back from the same person, company or source. Most people are so myopic (near sighted) that they look for the return immediately and expect it from the same person. When their giving does not immediately return to them, they believe the law isn't true and inescapable. This is a very short sighted perspective.

Imagine being in a sleeping bag in a log cabin up in the mountains where it is snowing. The evening air around you is so cold all you have out of the sleeping bag is your nose. It is so cold you can see your breath in the cabin. You then realize why it is so cold. There is no fire in the wood stove. You look around and notice there is no firewood in the cabin. All the wood is outside where it is snowing. It is so cold in the cabin you can't get your head out of the sleeping bag much less your whole body until it gets warmer. You try to make a deal with the stove. You tell the stove to warm you up and then you will gladly go outside and get the stove some wood. Ridiculous you say?! Yet how often do we live our life that way? In your relationship you say to the other person "You spend more time with me (stove warm me up) and I will be more loving or romantic to you (I'll get you some wood.)" Meanwhile the other person is thinking, "you be more loving or romantic and I will spend more time with you." In the average company, management is paying the employees just enough to keep them from quitting. The employees are working just hard enough to keep from getting fired. In our rush to not be taken advantage of, each of us is waiting for the stove to give us heat first

Solution number two is open, honest, responsible communication. Let's suppose someone is a half hour late for an appointment with you and so you become upset. You decide to apply this second solution and communicate with the person. It might sound like this, "I feel upset. I feel like you don't respect me when you don't keep your agreements. I am angry." Notice that all the communication is from ownership of your feelings. In saying "I am angry" you are owning or being responsible for your feelings. If you were to say, "You are making me angry" that would be non-responsible. You would have the viewpoint that something outside of yourself is at cause for your feelings. (We will be going into this viewpoint of responsibility in much greater depth in chapter four.) Very simply, you openly share your feelings without assigning the cause to someone else. This is often difficult because you may be afraid of their response. When you communicate responsibly it is not to change the other person's behavior. That would be nice, but often times the other person will not change. You are doing it so you don't hold onto your resentment and ultimately because you don't want to pay the negative prices for doing so.

When I was a child there were stamps people collected when they shopped at certain places. They were called S&H green stamps. As people collected them they placed them in a book and could trade in the filled books for certain awards. It was similar to today's frequent flyer programs. Many people treat their resentments like S&H green stamps. They don't say anything at the time of the resentment. They don't want to be rude or maybe they are simply afraid. But, they do put their resentment stamp in the book. Another resentment happens and they put it in the book. Eventually the book is full and they cash it in. This is when they blow up and there are serious consequences. You can avoid this and release the pressure valve along the way by communicating your feelings in a responsible way.

The third solution for handling resentment is called Fair Fighting. As best I can recall, this was developed by a psychologist out of Atlanta. It is very effective at resolving your resentment, however, it can only be used with someone you are in relationship with. It is great for parents and children, spouses, even with co-workers. The reason you must know the person is that you agree to fight according to set rules. Most people when they verbally fight, fight in a free for all. They end up saying and doing things that win the argument, but in the long term, lose the relationship. There are three rules each of you must agree to.

• **Rule #1** is you must agree on a code word or words. It might be "fight's on" or "red flag." It is simply a signal. When one of you calls it, you are reminded that you are going to fight by rules instead of however you might normally fight. It also puts out in the open that a fight is going to take place! Have you ever been in a fight, but you didn't know you were in a fight? You knew something was wrong, but you couldn't put your finger on exactly what was going on. You may not like it, but it is on the table in front of you.

• **Rule #2** is there are two minute rounds. One talks and the other listens. Whoever calls the code word first gets to talk first. For two minutes, they share their feelings and the other person does their best to not say anything and simply identify with the experience of the other person. They are not thinking of counter remarks or what they are going to say to defend themselves. They are doing the best they can to listen. At the end of two minutes, the roles are reversed. The fight can go however many rounds you want or need to fully communicate.

Communication is a two way process. It is sending and receiving. What rule #2 does is force both people to send and to receive. Some people are programmed as a child that when they get angry, they shut down and don't send their feelings. Other people are programmed to constantly outflow their feelings and they never receive. This rule forces both people to be in both modes. In my experience, it puts some perspective around the anger and reduces it. Have you ever had an argument that starts out with something like the socks thrown on the floor? Then, it goes to your mother-in-law. Then, it goes to what you did last year and then you are in World War III. When you fight fairly after two, three or maybe four rounds you might still be angry, but you won't have the intensity. You will be saying to yourself, "OK, I don't like their habit of throwing the socks on the floor, but it's not the end of our relationship". Remember to always communicate your feelings responsibly. There is no blame as you are simply sharing what you are experiencing.

• **Rule #3** is you both agree not to use any vulgarities. Vulgarities are words that are degrading put downs. They are a special sting aimed specifically at the other person. Many times, they are words that attack a person's physical body appearance, race, religion, ethnic origin. It is not foul language. The problem with vulgarities is because they have a sting to them, most people go directly to the 3R's when they receive a vulgarity. Their revenge is to say a vulgarity back that is a little worse. It then goes back and forth and is a sure fire way to ruin a relationship. You may say in the moment, "I hate you." But you would not call them a vulgar name.

Set the rules up and agree to them while everything is going well. Do not wait until you are in the heat of the moment and then bring out this book and suggest using these rules as you may find yourself eating this book. The rules may not even work the first few times you try them. You may call the code word "red flag" and the other person may say, "I'll show you a red flag—it will be your nose after I break it." Be patient with yourself anytime you are trying a new behavior. It is no different than learning a new skill like tennis. The first attempts will feel awkward, but once you get the hang of it, you will find it to be well worth the time spent.

These SOLUTIONS may not make logical sense.

Do not take my word for it nor go by your opinion. Simply use them and go by the results. Begin your pratice against the 3R's by thinking of the three people you have the most resentment towards and within one week give something nice to one, openly, honestly and responsibly, communicate with the other, and ask to set up fair fighting with the third. Do not be concerned with their response as this is not about them. They may get suspicious or refuse the gift. They may even ignore you.

These solutions are not so the person will like you or behave the way you want. This is not a manipulative maneuver to control them. It is a solution for you to begin releasing your 3R's and to stop you from paying the prices for being in the 3R's.

"Nobody can liberate you, but you."

Chapter Four
The Foundation of Liberty
RESPONSIBILITY

The Question: What if you were the cause of everything you experience?

There is a tiny desert dwelling animal called a sand wasp. It has a program or subconcious thinking that tells the sand wasp to place its food outside the opening to its burrow before it enters, and look around inside the burrow for anything dangerous. After finding nothing, the wasp brings the food inside its burrow and begins eating.

Let's add a scientist a few yards away hiding behind a cactus. As soon as the sand wasp enters the burrow, he races over and moves the food a few feet away from the entrance to the burrow, then runs back and hides behind the cactus. The sand wasp comes up and sees the food has been moved. It now pulls the food back over to the edge of the hole and goes back down to double check for danger. The scientist again runs over and pulls the food away from the hole and returns to hide behind the cactus.

The sand wasp comes up and sees the food has

been moved and now must pull the food back over to the edge of the hole and go back down and check for danger. The scientist yet again runs over and pulls the food away from the edge of the hole. The sand wasp comes up and sees the food has been moved. It pulls the food back to the edge of the hole and goes back to check for danger. How long would this continue? You can actually do this until the sand wasp dies! It will continue pulling the food back to the edge of the hole and drop over dead of starvation. A startling fact --- but Why? The sand wasp is totally victim to its programs. The genius of the human being is a God-given thing called **CHOICE**. The scientist could have said, " This is a dumb experiment, I quit." The truly sad thing is that most people are more like the sand wasp than the scientist. They give up their right of choice and defend their programs or beliefs to their grave. They say things like, "That's just the way I am", or "I've always been this way", or "I can't communicate my feelings, it's just not me." Ultimately, you must decide if you are a human being or a sand wasp.

The Lesson If you are looking for choice or options in life, it all begins with this concept.

Archimedes, the great Greek mathematician once said, "Give me a lever long enough, and I can move the world." This is the lever that is long enough to move your world to an incredible place of excellence. Let's approach this concept from the backdoor and start with a viewpoint called victim.

Victim: The viewpoint where something was done to you. You were exploited or taken advantage of. You were not in control.

Think of a time when you were in the victim role. Perhaps it was a car accident where the other person ran the red light or maybe it was a business deal where you were misled or they simply didn't do what they said they would. Perhaps it was a relationship you put your all into and they left. Bring a specific time to mind and allow yourself to re-experience it. What did you feel? Perhaps pain, anger, frustration, hopelessness, foolish or even stupid? Overwhelmed?

Now imagine looking at a U.S. nickel from the "heads" side. When asked to describe it, you would say that you saw the head of President Thomas Jefferson. If I then asked someone looking at the other side to decribe what they saw on the nickel, they would say that you were clearly mistaken. They may even ask, "Don't you see a picture of the Monticello building?" Of course you don't. This clearly illustrates two different viewpoints of the same coin, the front and the back. Sometimes, in our need to be right about our viewpoint we don't allow or even believe that other viewpoints also exist. One viewpoint does not mean another viewpoint must be wrong. They are simply two different viewpoints of the same thing.

This concept is much like the old story of five blind men who were taken to an object which was unknown to them and are asked to describe this object. One man says, it is a long, thick rope; Another says,

No, it is a massive wall;   The third says, no way, it is a pillar of great stone; The fourth one claims it to be a tarp and finally the fifth declares it to be a large lizard. Someone who could see explained that it was, in fact, an elephant. Each of the five men had been touching different parts of the elephant and as a result they had different viewpoints. It is the same with the two sides of the coin and with two viewpoints we call victim and responsible.

VICTIM VIEW   RESPONSIBLE VIEW

Victim is one viewpoint of the coin. Now, I'm going to ask you to take a deep breath and walk to the other side of the coin and the other side of the victim story you brought to mind. Instead of the victim viewpoint where it was done to you, look at your own story from the "tails" or responsible viewpoint.

Responsible: The viewpoint where you are "at cause" for your experience out of the choice or choices you have made.

Re-read that definition carefully. This is not fault or blame (a very different concept we will talk about later).

For example, let's say Roma, my wife, and I

had an argument. When I tell it from victim, it would sound like this, "She didn't listen to me," or "She called me a name." It would be about what she did to me. That's the victim viewpoint. When I tell it from responsible, I am begining to look at every choice I ever made which had anything to do with this situation.

It may be a choice which allowed the agrument to happen. Maybe it was a choice that set it up or that caused the argument to happen. Looking for such choices, I see choice number one: Who married my wife? Me! This doesn't mean I am at fault for the argument, but I could not have had a husband/wife argument if I had not chosen to marry my wife (one of the two best choices I ever made!).

Perhaps I chose, (again not consciously), to ignore some previous signals or remarks she made indicating she was tired. Again, the choices do not make me at fault, they are a cause for me having this experience. Perhaps I chose to work or travel a lot and she felt ignored by me. I probably could now see 100 choices I had made that were at cause for my experience. Again, not at fault, simply at cause for my having the experience.

Now, do your best to look for any and all the choices you ever made which have anything to do with the victim experience you initially brought to mind. Put some effort into this as it may not be easy. Go ahead, put this book down and take a couple of minutes to do this. (You may want to write these down.)

What did you experience when you looked at your story from the responsible viewpoint? There could be a variety of feelings that came from this perspective. You could have been surprised, resistant, excited, numb. Any number of wide-ranging experiences may occur in any circumstance. It is possible to experience many different things. When you operate in the mode of discovery, you can learn from any experience. Most people have a less emotional experience from the responsible viewpoint than from that of the victim.

Lesson number one with this topic: **Victim and responsible have nothing to do with the truth.** If you found yourself resistant to taking either viewpoint, repeat this to yourself. The different viewpoints have nothing to do with the truth, but everything to do with what we experience. If I look at a white shirt with dark green sunglasses (victim) it will look green. If I look at the white shirt with red sunglasses (responsible) it will look red. Does either one tell me what color the shirt really is? No, but the different sunglasses do have everything to do with what I experience about the shirt Victim and responsible have nothing to do with the truth, but everything to do with what we experience.

When you look at something from the victim viewpoint you will likely feel negatively (angry, pressured, foolish, sad etc.) and there is no hope for a solution. Simply defined, you cannot be victim and have a solution as well. However, when looking at it from the responsible viewpoint where you are at cause for your experience out of the choices you have made, solution becomes possible. This is a lot more exciting simply because there is the possibility that the situation can turn out how you would like. Now, is that a guarantee that when you look at it from responsible that the situation will turn out the way you want? No, but the odds do go up dramatically. From a zero chance of a solution with the victim viewpoint, it might go to a 50-50 chance of solution with a responsible viewpoint. Which odds do you want?

When you begin to look at everything from the responsible set of sunglasses, you feel better and there is more possibility of it turning out the way you want. The average person looks at everything from victim. They are victim to the economy, the weather, their schedule, their feelings, their bank book balance and all the other circumstances of life. A leader makes their decisions based on what matters rather than on the circumstances happening around them. Said another way, leaders let what really matters to them make their decision not what is necessarily convenient. For example, if a person were to say to you, "That exercise gave me a lot of value," are they coming from a victim or responsible viewpoint? It is victim. Why? They have said that the exercise is what was at cause instead of themselves. Anytime you assign anything other than yourself as being at cause for your experience, it is a victim viewpoint. Responsible would be to say, "I created a lot of value in that exercise." Remember, it is not what is true, but rather what the viewpoint creates as your experience.

We choose to see things from responsible because it is exciting and it creates the possibility of a solution. Hold yourself responsible for everything, not because it is true, but because of the possibilities that the viewpoint creates. Hold yourself responsible for the results in your life, not your parents or how you were raised or the company you work for. Choose to use the responsible viewpoint because of what you will create in your life as a result. Hold yourself responsible for how you feel, not what someone has said or done. Hold yourself responsible for how much money you make, not the economy, the size town you live in, your job. Hold yourself responsible for how the government is, the condition of the enviroment, for EVERYTHING! We at Klemmer and Associates have choosen to be responsible for creating " A world that works for everyone with no one left out." This is our mission not because of the truth but because of the excitement and possibilities we can see from the responsible viewpoint.

You cannot make someone responsible, because it is a viewpoint one has to choose to take. You cannot delegate responsibility, because responsibility is a viewpoint, something you choose. You can delegate authority, the right to make certain decisions. You can only encourage someone to view from responsible and then let them choose.

Responsibility does not mean that you are to blame or at fault. (This is a key distinction.) They are as different as houses and vegetables. If your map or subconcious thinking is that responsibility means fault, you will not look to see how you are responsible for anything, simply because no one wants to be at fault. Suppose my three children are running through the house in order of their ages. First the 20-year-old, then the 18 year-old and then ten steps behind our 12 year old. The 18-year-old sees the 20-year-old is getting away, lunges forward and knocks him down. The 20-year-old falls into the table knocking a glass of milk onto the floor. What is the first thing out of each child's mouth? "It's not my fault, Dad. He was chasing me." then... " it's not my fault, he was teasing me." and finally from the 12 year-old, "Its not my fault. I was just watching, Dad." It is OK for small children to come from this place. What is not OK is when they are a teenager or adult and still come from this viewpoint of fault or blame. Unfortunately in our society this is where most adults still operate from. If you doubt that, pick up your local big city paper. Choose any topic. Almost all the conversation will be about who is at fault. The realm of fault and blame offers no solutions. That is the true price that is paid for wearing that set of sunglasses.

What would be the responsible viewpoint in the analogy of the children running in the house? The 20-year-old could say, "I chose to run in the house where the milk was," because he did have other choices. He could have decked his brother or ignored him or even simply laughed at him. Responsibility is the viewpoint that my choices set up an experience, created the experience or allow it to happen. This does not mean the 20-year-old is at fault.

The 12-year-old could also look at it from responsible. Maybe she chose not to say anything to her brothers because she was afraid of being picked on. No fault, simply a choice. Even I, as the parent, made a thousand choices in this situation. I chose to have the children. I chose to raise my children in a fashion where it was OK to run in the house. I chose to be somewhere else at the time. None of these choices mean I was at fault. I gain power, possibilities and feel better when I choose the responsible viewpoint. If your experience around any event has anger, shame or guilt, you know you are still looking through who was at fault. You can do that, but you will pay the price of not moving forward, of stopping your growth.

Make a list of all the things you have been victim to in the last year. Start with the goals you set last year and did not make. Next, what did you allow yourself to be victim to? Perhaps you have been victim to your anger, to your lack of education or the amount of money you have. Make a list of at least ten experiences where you have been victim. If you cannot come up with at least ten places where you have been victim then add to the list what you are victim to in not being able to list your victim experiences. Now look at each event from the responsible viewpoint. You will likely struggle to see how you are responsible, that you had and still have choices. Is it possible there is something on your list that you cannot see where you were responsible --- where you had choices? Does that mean you are not responsible? No. Remember it is not about the truth. All it means is that you cannot yet see how you are responsible. Wherever you cannot see how you are responsible you have no power, no solutions, and you feel yucky.

I still struggle in certain circumstances to see how I am responsible. It is just a lot fewer places now than when I started this personal growth journey more than twenty years ago. The more I see how I am responsible for the fact that 40,000 people starve to death every day, the more things I can choose to do about it. Some of you who just read that last sentence said to yourself, "I don't want to think about how I am responsible for 40,000 people starving to death. I would feel terrible and depressed". This reaction simply means you are still not "seeing" what we are talking about as the responsible viewpoint. If I have a green pair of sunglasses and I try to see white through them what color does it seem? It looks green. If I try to see responsible through a victim set of sunglasses how would it come out? It would still look victim. Have you ever heard someone say I don't want to be more responsible? That is because they are looking at the topic with victim eyes. It changes this exciting empowering idea called responsible into a burden, a duty, an obligation, and it seems very heavy.

During one seminar, we had a gentleman travel all the way from China. He was a political figure and was charged with the authority to industrialize a particular section of China. His reason for attending the seminar was that he wanted to figure out how to industrialize that section of China without polluting it. For two days he did not say anything. Then I called on him and asked him to talk with me. He still didn't say anything. Then I realized that although he could understand a little English, he couldn't or was embarrassed to speak English. I asked him when he would choose to see how he was responsible for what he understood AND for what everybody else understood. He frowned. About 15 minutes later, it was as though a light bulb went off for him. I knew he had begun to see things differently or to pierce his set of sunglasses. He stood up and spoke Chinese. He had been going victim to the fact he didn't speak English.

He started to see he was responsible and began looking at his choices. He had decided to take the class. He chose not to bring a translator. He made lots of choices that set up and created the experience he was having. Now that he was looking from responsible, options opened up in front of him. One option was to simply speak Chinese! Now I had a problem. I could look at it from victim or I could look at it from responsible. The choices I had made to bring about this experience were many. I chose to have it in a location where people were more likely to come from Asia. I chose not to review the roster ahead of time. There were many, many choices.

Several hours later this man found a person who translated his Chinese to English for us and our English to Chinese for him. The ironic thing was that this person who became the translator had been in the room the entire time. When we look through victim, there are no options or solutions. Responsible opens up solutions and opportunities to us.

Another key distinction is that responsibility, accountability, and authority are all very different from each other. Many teenagers and adults confuse them. Authority is the right to make certain decisions. Accountability is the willingness to pay the price for your choices. Responsibility is the viewpoint that you have choices. People often want authority without being willing to be accountable. Teenagers often want the authority to decide when to come home without a curfew, but do not want to be accountable. Hitler's atrocities were partly a result of the fact that he told people they had the authority to do certain things, but that he was accountable and responsible. If you have followed what has been said, you cannot give up responsibility because it is the viewpoint where your choices create your experience. Anytime the prices for a responsible viewpoint are really high, it is easy to pretend we don't have any choices. We always have choices. It is often that the consequences are high for our choices. When K & A works with teenagers, we tell them they don't have to go to school. In the beginning most of them argue. They say they have to. Anytime you feel you "have to," know that it is victim to believe there are no choices. The teens begin to realize they could choose not to go to school. The price they would pay might be to go to jail, but they could still choose that. There is a whole different experience one has when one even starts to say " I choose to" and instead of "have to". Where in your life do you feel you "have to" do something? Try saying "I choose to" and keep saying it. You will begin to have a different experience while doing the same "have-to" as before. You might even begin to see other choices and decide that the price isn't as high as you once thought and instead choose to do things differently.

"Reality is for those who lack imagination."

Chapter Five
To Think is To Create

The Question: Do you think?
Or does your thinking think you?

There once was a man who washed *The Story* windows for a living. He wasn't very happy so he went to a positive thinking-pep-rally-motivational type of seminar. He got positive and motivated. He went back to his job and was washing windows on the 15th floor. He was saying to himself, "I am a great window washer. I am a fantastic window washer. I am an incredible window washer." While he was shouting these affirmations to himself his scaffolding broke. Being 15 stories high he started falling, much like the cartoon character Wiley Coyote. About the third floor, as he continued down, a couple on the third floor heard this positive thinking window washer yelling, "So far so good! So far so good!" The moral of the story is that he still fell to the ground despite all his positive thinking.

A simple way to state the philosophy *The Lesson* we have been discussing is "To Think is to Create". While it appears to be a simple statement, it is not an easy one to fully understand. You may have already heard it many different ways before. The Bible states in Proverbs 23:7 "As a man thinketh in his heart so is he". Napoleon Hill said that "Whatever the mind of man can conceive and believe, it can achieve." Or Robert Allan's "As a man thinketh". The problem is that until you truly internalize it - you will not create your life anymore differently than you have already.

What does thinking really mean? In the story of the window washer, his thinking positively did not create a new reality of not crashing to the ground. This is not to say that positive thinking is not a good thing, because it is. It just doesn't quite go far enough to create results in the way we mean results. If you have a child on drugs, positive thinking will not be enough. If all it took for people to be financially wealthy was positive thinking, the world would have a lot more financially wealthy people. In order for us to explore this fundamental premise in Personal Mastery let's look at another diagram of a person that will help explain the different levels of thinking and what is meant by "To Think Is To Create".

Imagine a diagram similar to a snow person made up of three levels. The levels can be called many different names. It is important to not allow yourself to get hung up in the words, but rather begin to play detective and explore for yourself the idea and concepts of each level. The first level has been called the head, the conscious mind, the lower-self and other names. This level consists of reason, logic, and your five physical senses. Yet have you ever woken up to an alarm clock? If you were asleep, who heard the alarm clock? (I know some of you are saying your spouse! But, if you were alone—who heard it?) Obviously you heard it, so there has to be at least two levels to you—one that goes to sleep and one that doesn't sleep. The first level or concious mind is the one that goes to sleep. The number two level or subconcious is the one that never goes to sleep and hears the alarm clock and wakes you up.

Now you will notice there is a third level in our snowperson drawing. Unlike the first two levels which are circles, the third level is drawn as a half circle. That is to indicate the infinite versus the first two circles which are finite. I choose to call this third and infinite level God. You may choose to call it another name. The universe, the super concious, these are names often given to this level. One of the lessons I learned from my children is that the name they call me—Pops, Dad, Father, Step Dad or even Old Man—is not necessarily as important as the attitude with which they speak to me. You can label this third, infinite level with whatever name you choose.

How then does, "To Think Is To Create," relate to this new diagram of you? The story of the positive thinking window washer at the begining of this chapter clearly illustrates that positive thinking is not the thinking I am referring to.

The window washer was thinking with his number one level or his conscious mind. Concious thinking rarely changes the outcome much. To check this out, think real hard and actually say out loud, "I am the President of the United Nations." Did this number one level thinking make you President of the United Nations? Simply thinking with your concious mind does not create in reality the results you say you want. It seems to take something more powerful than simple reason and logic.

"To Think Is To Create" refers to your thinking at the number two level. Here is where your deep-seated assumptions about who you are, how life works, what YOU think success is or what it takes to be successful exist. This is the level with your sunglasses, the maps of your subconcious thinking that we referred to. Do you think experience happens to you or do you think you create it? Do you think you are a body or something more? It is not what is true, it is what you think is true, your fundamental beliefs that determine your idea of what your reality is for you. Whether the world is flat or round does not determine the decision you make about traveling, it is how you think the world is that determines your decision about traveling. When people thought the world was flat they didn't go far. When they thought it was round they ventured much farther. Whether the world is truly a risky or safe place does not determine your actions, but rather what you believe the world to be and how well you believe you are capable of handling it that determines what you will do and where you will travel.

Try the following simple exercise to illustrate this further and allow us to explore in more depth how our thinking creates our reality. Take a piece of paper and write your full name on it as many times as you can with your non-writing hand in 60 seconds. Then and only then continue reading. What did you experience? Some people did not do the excercise, some did it, but didn't go very fast. Some were very competitive - some were not. Some worried about consistency, some did not. Some had fun and some thought it was stupid while others were unmoved during the exercise. What did YOU feel? What caused you to feel that way? I cannot tell you what caused you to feel that way. I can tell you several viewpoints or ways of looking at it and what my own experience or viewpoint is.

When I do this "live" with people I keep telling them how many seconds are left, to keep going faster and then I count down the last few seconds. When I ask what caused the feelings some people will say they were irritated by my tone of voice or uncomfortable using their non-writing hand. Others will say "I felt pressure because you were counting down the time." The interesting thing is someone else will say "I didn't experience pressure, I was simply curious to see what this exercise was about." Yet someone else will say they felt totally freed up and didn't even worry what they were going to do. Therefore if what you experience is a result of what you are doing how could it be that everyone just did the same thing but experienced very different things?

I am proposing **there are two fundamental ways people think about the way the world is.** One is that what you or someone else is doing is what creates your experience. Most people think this way. Listen to people today. They will say, "of course I'm upset, my boss just yelled at me." Their viewpoint or set of sunglasses is that what someone is doing is creating their experience. It is as though the boss yelling at them created their upsetness. "Of course I'm feeling insecure—I just lost my job". As if losing your job has anything to do with how you feel—most people think it does.

Belief #1   Doing = Experience
Belief #2   Thinking = Experience

The majority of people as we have just discussed believe #1 is the way the world is. The problem with this belief is that if that is truly the way of the world— you are stuck. Unless the circumstances change, you will have a certain experience. End of discussion. Based on the simple exercise of a room full of people all doing the same thing —the above name writing exercise—many having different experiences, I believe that belief #2, our thinking at the number two level, is actually what creates our reality. These beliefs at our number two level create our experience not only of whether we are happy or frustrated, but what our bank balance is, whether we are single or married, which job we are in, and all other aspects of our life. The good news is that with the subconcious creating our experience, we have much greater potential to change our thinking than we do to change circumstances or other people.

How do you change your thinking at the number two level? It's easy and simple. Actresses, Scientists and Professional Athletes all do it; Artists do it; Chief executives do it; Religious leaders do it; Good students do it; but do you do it? What is it? The answer is visualization and yes you do it. Everyone does. It is the only language of the number two level, your subconscious. The real question is whether you use it unconsciously, meaning with no guidance by your number one level or whether you consciously apply the use of visualization. The choice becomes one of whether you want your odds of success to be those of a lottery or do you want them stacked in your favor. If you don't apply visualization consciously then your subconscious will apply it according to your beliefs and you will recreate what you already have.

The reason visualization or imagination is so powerful is that it works at your number two level. People of certain religious persuasions sometimes categorize imagination as strictly a "new age" thing. In reality it is something which all religions use. They simply apply it in different ways and toward different ends. In 1996, I attended a Christian leaders conference in Hawaii run by Harrison International Seminars. It was fantastic and we now attend every year. In 1996 I was privileged to speak and the speaker after me was Oral Roberts. He spoke for an hour and a half on visualization. Regardless of your prejudices about him, positive or negative, he is a well read Bible expert. Visualization is neutral and can be seen much like money which can be applied for good, such as building a home, or bad, such as drugs.

I interviewed an Olympic athlete and previous world record holder, Marilyn King. She said, "No athlete in their right mind would attempt to compete at this elite level without using some form of visualization." Scientists like Thomas Edison, were well documented as having used visualization and imagination to invent. Visualization is different than imagination. Visualization is reproducing a picture in your mind of something you have seen. Look at the floor you have your feet on right now. Close your eyes and see the floor. That's visualization. Some people can see in detail yet for others it's a blur. In either case, this is visualization. Now imagine a carpet made totally of chocolate. This is imagination. (Presuming you have never seen a chocolate carpet before.) Imagination is creating a picture of something you have never seen. Again, some see a lot of details, like the indentation marks of a Hershey Bar, others see a brown blur. In either case, this is imagination, because you have not actually seen a chocolate carpet.

How do you consciously apply visualization? There are many methods and books around this subject and I suggest you may want to read them. For this book I will keep it simple. Athletes simply see a picture of themselves throwing a perfect pass or sacking the quarterback. They often call it mental rehearsal. You can do it with an upcoming job interview or in completing a sale or even for the perfect interaction between you and your child. Negative visualizing is called fear. You are visualizing an outcome you don't want and having an emotional reaction.

One of the simplest methods for visualizing is called Screen of the Mind. Visualize a movie screen or a television screen. Now imagine it is surrounded by a dark border. Now, on the screen, visualize the situation as it is now. For example, let's say you are renting an apartment, but want to own a home. You would see yourself in your apartment. Just like it really is. All of this is on a screen with a dark border. I like to picture it surrounded with lights, like on a vanity mirror and the lights are turned out. Perhaps you just want to use a dark picture frame or just paint around the TV screen in a dark color. Next you change the frame to a light color and on the screen put an image of what you want. For our example, you would turn all the lights around the vanity mirror on or change it to a light picture frame. On the screen you would see yourself living in a three bedroom house writing out the mortgage check with a big smile on your face. That's all there is to it.

You could be interviewing for a job and you would see yourself being turned down on a screen with a dark border and then getting accepted on a screen with a light border. Some people ask why the dark border first. For myself it has to do with the fact that the subconcious always wants to see the pictures it believes are reality before it accepts a new or replacement vision.

Visualize a big street motorcycle. Imagine you want to go to the top of a hill, but your motorcycle has died. Can you imagine pushing this dead motorcycle up a hill? A lot of work. Now visualize that you point the motorcycle downhill. You let it roll a little ways to build momentum and then you change its attitude (or direction) to point uphill. The momentum now carries you uphill in the direction you want. It is much like that with your mind. If you weigh 200 pounds and want to weigh 150 pounds there will be a normal resistance for your mind to see you at 150 pounds. Let your subconcious go the way it wants for a short period seeing you at 200 pounds on a screen with a dark frame, then simply change the direction by putting a light frame around the screen with your vision of weighing 150 lbs. First build momentum and then point your thinking in the direction you want. This is not a totally clean physics analogy (if you are a physics buff), but it explains the principle well.

As you are sowing these new pictures of what you want, your subconcious (your number two level) will go to work creating the solutions. In the case of our weight analogy you will find yourself being more disciplined, making different food choices, leaving food on your plate when you are full maybe even getting more exercise. In the case of buying a house you will find yourself discussing different options to finance a house where before you weren't even open, or even seemingly out of the blue, someone will want to invest money and starts looking at a partnership. Do you have to figure all of this out? Do you have to know how you will get to the new vision? No. That is the job of your number two level. It is the problem solving part of you. Unfortunately though, most people try and solve all their problems or challenges with their number one level— their reason and logic. Level number one has an important function, but it is not to solve problems.

Have you ever been to a Circus? Have you seen a man or woman riding an elephant? They tap the elephant with a stick and it turns left. They tap the elephant and he moves a boulder. They tap him and he bends his head down. Which has more raw power, the elephant or the adult? The elephant! It's not even a contest. What would happen if the adult says, "I'm the big cheese, you sit in the tent, I'll do all the work today?" The adult wouldn't accomplish very much and they would end their day bushed, tired out. Yet this is the way most human beings are. Why? Because they have left their elephant, their number two part, in the tent. Your number two level really is your problem solver.

Did you ever hear "What you sow, so shall you reap"? This applies internally as well as externally. The number two level will produce weeds or flowers based on what you sow. Reason and logic and your five physical senses are what reside in the number one level. This is why level one is sometimes referred to as the head. It can solve very little and yet it is where our education is most often focused. For example, someone who wants to buy a house tries to solve the question of how with their head, their reason and logic. They look at their income, then they look at their outflow if they should buy the house. If the income doesn't surpass the outflow they don't buy the house. This is often where average and mediocre thinking stops.

Now what if the elephant said, "I'm doing whatever I like doing. You stay in the tent Mr. or Mrs. Adult." You would have chaos, and a wild bull elephant on the loose. This is just what happens when people send their conscious mind out to lunch, by taking drugs or too much alcohol. In essence, your subconcious thinking or your programs are unrestrained and much of this thinking is not normally supportive of us being all we want to be.

You can also use visualization to get guidance. You can see yourself asking a question of Jesus or whoever your religious figure is or even of someone you respect, such as your father or a well-respected business person. What if they aren't alive? Not a problem. Strange you say? Not at all. Have you ever had an argument with someone while you were driving a car only no one else was in the car? It was in your mind and you were using this principle to the negative.

Many times when you ask a question of someone

in your mind you will have an answer. There really is no one in your head giving you the answer. It is merely your number one level talking to your number two level and back again. You are having a conversation with yourself using the language of the number two level which is visualization. Psychologists today say conversation is occurring all day long, but we are unaware of it because our focus is on the outer objective world. Have you ever been in a room and not heard the air conditioner until you focused on it? Visualization is very much the same way of bringing attention to what you want and desire as results in your life. It is focusing on and directing the conversation for the purpose of getting new ideas to your conscious mind. Visualization is a way of circumventing the filters of your prejudices, beliefs, and even your programs.

Imagination and visualization are keys which open up the door to your elephant. To be a Master at anything, one practices. A Master musician or athlete does not practice once in awhile or only when they feel like it. They practice everyday, regularly, and consistently and often at the same time and same place. They are disciplined and you must be too, if you aspire to walk in Mastery and create a life of liberty.

Make a commitment right now to consciously practice visualization everyday at a certain location for at least the next 30 days. Do a mental rehearsal of the day going the way you want and you achieving your year goals. Practice and see what actually begins to occur for you and judge this simple exercise on the results you create while in the practice of it.

"He who knows why
will always employ
he who knows how."

Chapter Six
Your Vision

The Question: What is the point to your life?

The Story

One day while working for Tom, he asked to see my life plan. I told him I didn't have one. He told me to go out to my car and get it. I told him that what I meant was that I had not written out a life plan. He complained that I didn't listen to him. Tom had written a book, "Living Synergistically" where he had said to write your own life plan. I had interpreted that as being a metaphor or conceptual. (At least that sounded better than my being too lazy or undisciplined to write it out.) He muttered a few words I won't repeat and then said, "OK, show me your five year plan." I told him I didn't have one of those either. He muttered a few more words about expecting more out of me. Tom then said "At least you wrote some new years resolutions out and have a one year plan!" Embarrassed, I explained that I had set a few goals in my head, but that I hadn't written any down. Tom told me to go home and not come back to work until I had a written life plan. I had never had a boss do this kind of thing, but I was smart enough to figure out that if I didn't do well at this, it could become a permanent vacation.

After a couple of days I returned with several written pages and showed them to Tom. I will never forget the look on his face. He looked at what I had written and asked with a furrowed brow, " What is this?" I replied that that was my life plan. " This is your life plan?!" I repeated that it was. By now I was frustrated and confused. I had put what I thought was a lot of work into this and it was apparent that something was wrong. He said, "This only goes out 50 years?" I explained I was only 27 and I figured that 77 was a good life. He then not so gently said that I obviously didn't get anything. Now I was in the 3R's talked about in Chapter 3.

The questions Tom asked next challenged my way of thinking about goal setting. Do you think you are a physical body? Is that why you are only setting goals for as long as you think that body will last? Don't you get that you have a body, but that is not who you are? You are a spiritual being in temporary possession of a physical body. If you understood that you would be setting goals for 100 years, 500 years, for eternity. Even if you can't see that vision, at least you must see that you have an effect on your family, community, the world long after your phsical body has rotted and is feeding worms. At least you would set goals for 100 years because of the effect you will have. What kind of a game do you want to play with your life, a big one or a small one? Do you want a week to week game like most people or a five hundred year game? Let me tell you that experience totally changed my set of sunglasses about goal setting.

The size of your goals will have a huge effect on your activities, what you do and your persistence or willingness to pay the prices necessary to achieve those goals. If you don't have big dreams you will not be willing to pay big prices to achieve them.

In the previous chapter we mentioned a gentleman who traveled all the way from China to Hilo, Hawaii to take a seminar with me. Why? He had the authority to industrialize a section of Communist China and he wanted to industrialize it without polluting the area. He came to the seminar to solve that challenge.

How's that for a big dream? I was impressed. That big dream is what allowed him to pay big prices such as the travel cost and inconvenience of going somewhere where he didn't speak the language as well as the price of taking seven days out of his busy life. If you don't have a big dream you won't pay big prices!

We have a division of Klemmer & Associates where all our clients are network marketing companies and their representatives. I tell the representatives that one of the most important things to do before they allow a new person to sign on is to assist that person to discover a big dream. Otherwise the minute the new person meets the rejection that you know they will meet in building the business, they will quit. People with big dreams are willing to endure this rejection. We ask major Fortune 500 clients of ours, who want to undergo reorganizing—Why? What's their big dream? Because we know there will be turmoil and resistance along with the change. If they don't have a big dream they will give up and go back to the old way of doing things.

But there is something even bigger than the size of your dream which affects your daily activities—the why behind the goal. This is your vision. We could explore the why behind your individual goals and I do recommend that you do that, but let's cut to the chase.

Why are you living? What is the point? Are you living just to survive? If you are—that's kind of funny because that's a losing battle. After all, at somepoint you are going to die. Are you living just for fun? Fun comes and goes. The search for fun as your end result, leads to emptiness. I do not know your purpose. You need to discover it, if you want the fire and passion in life. Part of my interpretation of the Proverbs quote "a people without a vision, perish" is that an individual, company, a nation, anything without a vision, slowly dies. They either become emotionally dead—numb—financially dead, or actually physically die. Talk to an insurance agent about the length of time for the average man to live after he retires. I have been told it's less than three years and though there are exceptions, that is the average. Maybe the reason for this statistic is that many men have retirement as their goal and when they reach it they forget to set another goal to visualize beyond retirement.

How many times have you seen someone raise themselves up out of a disadvantaged situation to play a pro sport? They had a big dream and they accomplished it, only to return to bad circumstances when they left sports. They forgot to have a dream beyond the dream. How do you get a big dream? There are three keys. **Key number one** is to start with whatever your biggest dream is at the moment. I learned in an interview I did with Wally Amos who founded Famous Amos Cookies that, he didn't start with a global vision. He started with a dream of one store being the best there was in the area and the dream developed from there. Don't compare your dream to others. If you do, you will lose the joy in the journey. **Key number two** is that for the moment don't worry about whether it is "the right dream." You can change it at anytime. Imagine you are a ship in the harbor and you won't leave the harbor because you can't make up your mind whether to go to England or Spain. Now imagine you pick England, leave the harbor and one thousand miles out to sea switch your goal to Spain. You are far better off than if you were still waiting in the harbor trying to decide.

I can remember saying to myself, "God, I know I'm good (yes, I was arrogant) but, you have got to tell me what to do." I didn't think I heard him, so I did nothing. Then one day I got some feedback just to get started and He would reveal the plan, just get some momentum. I thought I'd get involved with a local politician to make a difference. After awhile, I realized that doing the Personal Mastery seminars was really the vehicle for me to make a difference. I was further along than if I had stayed at home and not worked for the politician. Which brings us to **key number three**. Open up to God for your vision. Thanks to a student of one of my seminars, Jeff Chatsworth, who is now a friend, I got a bit more insight. He was using a NIV bible. He said I was misquoting by saying vision because the NIV uses the word "revelation". I was using the King James Bible which goes "A man without vision perishes". Revelation is revealing what already exists. It is actively seeking out God's will, (or whatever you call Him or Her in your particular religious doctrines.) But how do you do that? By quieting out the noises of the physical world we live in and praying or meditating.

So pick a vision and get your feet moving. Now what is the difference between vision and goals? To give the dictionary definition—Vision is purpose—the Why. Goals are objectives that we either achieve or not. Vision is like direction. It's never ending. Goals are finite in that we either accomplish them or we don't. Activities are defined as the things we do. Take a look at the diagram below:

In my experience most people are activity oriented (75%). The husband is about what he needs to do—call someone, take the kids to the school, make a sales call, etc. The same is true with a wife, boss, employee. A small percentage (perhaps 20%) are goal oriented. Ask a married couple for a marriage goal.

Maybe 1 of 5 will have one. Most are simply doing the marriage. Ask people for an income goal for this year or five years. Many don't have one, they simply are doing their job. Goal-oriented people achieve goals. So set goals and write them down. NOW!

Write your life story out. By that I mean write your 1 - 5 - 10 - 20 - 50 - 100 - 500 year goals. You might be laughing, but I ask you, "How big a game do you want to play?" It's up to you. However, if you stop at goal orientation you will likely burn out. Do you know someone in burnout? Most likely they were goal oriented. They set a goal of making $50,000 a year. They made it. Then they set a goal of $100,000 a year. They made it. They set a goal of $150,000 a year. They made it. At some point they burn out. Why? Because they have lost sight of WHY they were settings the goals.

What is their purpose or vision? Why are they making the money? The why is the fuel that powers the goals. In training our facilitators, their first assignment is to write down all the whats that we do and then they must figure out why we do them. Why do we have the chairs set up the way we do? Why do we tell a particular story and why do we tell it when we do? If you know the why, and the circumstances change, you can adjust what you are doing and still fulfill the original purpose. If you only know what to do, you are stuck doing the what even if it isn't fulfilling the original purpose or even if it isn't working anymore. With the above chart, you want to start from the top down. If you have a vision, will you set goals? Yes. If you set goals, will you decide on activities to achieve those goals? Yes. And they will all line up and you will have INTEGRITY.

If you start from the bottom up you may not get to the top and if you do, they may not line up. There will not be integrity between the different levels and you will feel unfulfilled. You may be a great doctor or parent or teacher but, feel unfulfilled because those things do not support your purpose. This is one of the reasons organizations are strong on mission statements. Many people today are spending years earning money in order to be secure only to learn money does not guarantee security. I personally know people with an excess of a million dollars in their portfolio and they are afraid of losing it. They are still insecure. They did not have the alignment or integrity between their vision, goals and activities that we are talking about. They have not examined the why and whether what they are doing will fulfill that why. Some of the best work I have ever read regarding vision is by Richard Brooke, CEO of Oxyfresh. Be sure to pick up his book *Mach II With Your Hair on Fire* and don't let the strange title deceive you. It is a well-written book by a person with results, that from my viewpoint is must reading.

Let's talk about activity for a moment. Even in activity there is activity and productivity. List all the activities you did yesterday. Stop reading this book and do it now on the top of the next page:

Now examine each activity and decide which were productive (produced income or moved you to results) and which was simply activity—busy work. Put a check mark by each one that was productive. How much of your time was spent productively and how much was spent on busy work?

Often an entrepreneur will tell me they are working hard but not making any money. We explore how they are spending their time and much of it usually is in busy work. They are playing "office" versus creating customers. They are making plans, doing brochures, organizing file cabinets, creating a business card, etc. instead of picking up the phone and setting an appointment with a potential customer. Are you committed to activity or productivity? Do you have your activity aligned with your goals and your vision? How big is your game?

*"Balance is the key
to power and
peace of mind"*

Chapter Seven
Balance

The Question: Where do you spend more time, in the bathroom or communicating with loved ones?

Visualize a rectangular block of wood 2 inches wide by 2 inches deep and 10 inches tall. On top of the block stands a wire figure of a man. The feet are fine points. In each hand the figure is holding a round ball. When you push on the figure in any direction it rocks back and forth, but it never falls off. It is balanced in such a way that it always recovers.

Visualize a 75 watt light bulb. The same amount of energy it takes to power that very light bulb will also cut through 6 inches of steel! No extra power is required, but it does need it to be focused in the form of a laser.

Focus is a key to results and is often perceived as a contradiction to balance, but that does not have to be so. (Balance is the key to maintain power and long term peace of mind.) Balance and focus together produce maximum results.

In the previous chapter you examined your vision, the "why" you are living. As you begin to set up the goals or objectives that will support you in creating that vision, I recommend that you do it with a sense of balance. Do you have a body? Yes. That's one of the easy questions. What other natures or bodies do you suppose you have other than just your physical body? Do you have a feeling nature? Of course you do, you have emotions. What about a mental nature? How about a spiritual nature? (Not necessarily a religious dogma—but some connection to a higher power, an infinite being-whatever word you choose.)

There is an old notion that you and I are like a square (and you spent years trying to be hip or cool—at least we baby boomers did!). It suggests we have four sides: physical, emotional, mental, and spiritual. What makes a square a square though, is that all four sides are equal and they are at right angles to each other. The idea is that when all four of our natures are developed equally we are in balance. This balance leads to both an inner contentment or peace of mind as well as power in our lives. Unfortunately, due to family, societal and other influences, we often do not develop equally on all four sides.

I'm not actually saying that you are the square. You are not your physical body. You just happen to live in one. Perhaps you aren't your emotions or your thinking either. This then leads us to an ageless question. Who are you? This a great question and is deserving of your attention and effort.

Before taking on this question of who you really

are, let's use this square to do a quick self-evaluation. Draw a line from 1 to 10 and rate your physical side— your health. A 10 would be perfect weight, endurance, blood pressure, etc and one is the low end—terrible health, sick all the time or very bad blood pressure. Five would be average. Give yourself an honest rating (go ahead, no one is looking).

Now, rate yourself on your emotional or feeling nature. How is your self expression of your emotions? A ten would be perfect self expression of your feelings; You are always understood. You can clearly express a wide range of feelings at anytime. A one on the scale would be terrible at communicating your feelings and you have either totally suppressed your feelings, are numb and unable to get them out of your mouth or you are wildly out of control of the expression of your feelings. Five is average. Honestly give yourself a rating.

Next rate yourself in the area of mental development. Some people choose to rate this by the amount of formal education. When I first did this, I started to give myself a very high number because I had a West Point education, had made the Dean's List frequently, and had a Master's Degree. My mentor asked me if I was smart. I thought I was. Then he asked why, if I was so smart, wasn't I rich and why I didn't have the romantic relationship I wanted. Although I didn't like it, I saw that I had lots of data in my head, but this didn't mean I was mentally developed. On the mental side, I gave myself a five because I think there are other things to look at in order to evaluate your mental development, and education is but a small part of it.

Your income might be a part of your evaluation in this area. If you are earning $500,000 per year and have a net worth over a million dollars or a passive cashflow that exceeds your expenses then give yourself a 10 in the mental area. If you can't make your monthly bills you might rate yourself more in the area of a 1. You might also use the size of the problem you can solve. If you can solve global problems give yourself a ten. If you can't even solve your attitude for the day, give yourself a one. Honestly rate yourself.

Lastly rate your spiritual development. A ten would be where you have a terrific relationship with your creator or higher power. You know your purpose in life and you are fulfilling it. You always come from a "we" standpoint and see your connection to the rest of humanity. You are making sure others win as well as you. A one on the scale would be where you think your life is all about you and what you get out of it. It is where you don't know your purpose or even that you could have one. Honestly rate yourself on your spiritual development.

Begin to put the four numerical evaluations together by drawing a vertical line on the right hand side of the page in proportion to the number you gave yourself for your physical development. If you gave yourself an eight it would be quite long, perhaps six inches on a page this size. If you gave yourself a small number such as a two, then make it much shorter. Perhaps only an inch & half long. Now, draw a line on the bottom from the right to left in proportion to the rating you gave yourself for emotions. Now come up the left vertically with a line proportional in size to the number you gave yourself for mental development. Lastly come across the top from the left to right with a line proportional to your spiritual mark development.

Below is the way my square came out the first time I did this in 1975.

I gave myself a seven physically. I was in the army running three miles a day and in pretty good shape. On the emotional side I gave myself a two. I grew up where strength

meant suppression of your feelings. It was not OK to be angry. You did not ever say "I love you". I was what is sometimes referred to as a stoic. My emotional side was not very developed. I probably was a bit too generous with a two rating, but I didn't want to look too bad! I gave myself a zero on the spiritual side because I had grown up with—"it's a dog eat dog world"—if you don't look out for yourself, no one else will. The Vietnam War was recently ended and I was cynical. If there was a God then he was doing a terrible job. I didn't have a purpose I was conscious of, so I simply said zero. Don't compare yours to mine. Simply be honest with youself. Do it now in the space below.

Some of you will have a balanced square and some won't. Mine, as you can see, was very out of balance. Where do you suppose most of my goals were at that time? More physical fitness and nutrition; more degrees in education. Not that this is bad, but it was driving me more out of balance. I was putting in more and more effort and getting less results—the law of diminishing return.

After this exercise I set self expression (emotional), relationship, and spiritual goals. What happened? I became more contented with an internal peace of mind and coincidentally my income doubled. It was as though I had been stretching like a rubber band in only one direction and yet I needed to be balanced before my life could expand. Once I began to stretch the shorter areas of my life I experienced growth and expansion in all areas.

For some the square is already very balanced. A baby is very balanced. 1 - 1 - 1 - 1. Life is about growth in all areas. The question, if your square is balanced at perhaps 7 - 7 - 7 - 7, is "how can you stay balanced and grow in all areas?" If you get to I0 - I0 - I0 - I0, you'll probably discover the scale now goes to 100. Life is a journey—not a destination and there are ways to grow and expand ourselves.

Let's talk about growth and relationships for a moment, using this model. Suppose you were a man who grew up where muscles were important. You were popular and got the pretty girl this way and education and money were highly valued. You were going to be the bread winner and money talked, the rest walked. I'm not saying it's you and I'm not stereotyping all males. Let's just take someone who grew up like this. His square could look like the following diagram.

Now, let's take a woman who grew up where feelings were important, intuition and a spiritual nature valued and was told don't get too many muscles—the boys won't like you - and don't be too smart. Maybe her brother went to college, but there wasn't enough money for her to go. I'm not saying all woman are this way and I'm not saying even most woman are this way. Let's just look at one person who grew up this way:

The man and woman meet and yet hey don't live happily ever after. Why? Take a look at how their squares overlap:

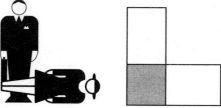

Not a lot of overlap. They only relate to each other in the overlapping area. He comes from reason and logic and says to her "You don't make any sense." She comes from feelings and says, "Why can't you feel what I am talking about?"

If either one expands their square along the shorter sides the new square will encompass more of the other person. They can relate more and have a better relationship—even if the other person does not choose to grow. If they both grow, then the quality of the relationship expands exponentially and is enriched.

Take the time, right now to write down your own goals for each side. As many as you can. Don't get stuck on which side it belongs in, just start building your list and put them on the side that best describes the goal from your viewpoint.

Chapter Eight
Oneness vs. Separateness

The Question: What if your boss and you were connected with an umbilical cord?

 **In** 1985 I did a workshop for several religious leaders. There were 53 individuals of various theologies: Catholic Priests, Jewish Rabbi's, Mormon, Pentecostal, Methodist, Unity, Seventh Day Adventist, and several others. At the beginning they thought I was going to talk theology with them. Instead, we talked about what mattered to them (preaching the word better, happier home lives, less stress, growing their congregation, etc). They explored what beliefs they had that prevented them from achieving what mattered to them. All of them professed great love and yet in the beginning of our workshop some of them would not sit next to each other. They all talked about mankind as one family and yet many of them began the seminar as if I and they were each combatants to be convinced of the others viewpoint. In one exercise on leadership, one group literally laughed at the other group for not listening or seeing that the excercise could have had a win-win resolution. Then they realized that in that moment they were in judgment and separating themselves from the other group, which is not win-win.

The difference between the truth of what we actually believe and what we think we believe is often a harsh awakening. After piercing this veil or set of sunglasses about separateness and what they really believed, amazing behaviors occurred. After one break, a Seventh Day Adventist Minister and a Jewish Rabbi shared that they had a conversation about how neither of their children could participate in the community soccer league. They both celebrated their holy day on Saturday. They decided to form a joint Jewish-Seventh Day Adventist soccer league that played on Sundays.

| **The Lesson** | **Win-Win** is becoming a popular buzz word for a very old idea. Steven |

Covey made it very popular in his book, *7 Habits of Highly Effective People*. Buckminister Fuller did ground breaking work on this topic as well. Martin Luther King in his speeches talked about all races having food, shelter, and living in harmony, not just the black race. Mahatma Ghandi worked on peace for the British, Indian, Hindu, and Seiks. These world leaders believed in win-win thinking.

So why aren't more people win-win oriented? I believe it is because a fundamental assumption about reality for most people is that we are separate. You see your body growing up and it appears separate from others. One appears male, the other female. Once this set of sunglasses or subconcious thinking called separateness is in place, it filters everything through an us and them way of seeing the world. Christian vs. Muslim, Conservative vs. Liberal, rich vs. poor, talkative and shy, old and young, Americans and non-Americans.

Once this way of thinking is in place, no matter how many teamwork books you read or posters on the topic you have, you will not approach life from a win-win veiwpoint. It will be labor versus management or my department versus your department. Individuals will fight over limited resources. As we talked about in Chapter 3, our behavior is determined by our programs or subconcious thinking and not —**NOT** by what we want, **OR** even what we know is good for us, and definitely **NOT** by what we are told to do.

Imagine two islands. One is the beautiful island of Maui and the other is a much smaller more barren island known as Ka'ho'olawe. Ka'Ho'olawe is not inhabited and for many years was used as a bombing range by the military. If you and I were sailing down the channel between them they would look different. One is tall, the other is short. One is lush, the other relatively barren. One is populated, one isn't. One is lively, the other is dead. One is near, the other is far. There would be a long list of differences.

Suppose we pulled a plug on the ocean like a bath tub. We let the water level drop 100 feet and put the plug back in. Now as we look at the two islands they appear more similar. They are not exactly the same, but they are closer in color, size, distance, saftey, etc. Now, imagine we drain all the water out of the ocean. What do we discover? It is all one island. This is what we call the reality of oneness versus the illusion of separateness. I'm not saying the islands aren't separate, because at the top they are. But, where is most of an island, below the water line or above? Below. Where you can see or where you can't see? Where you can't see. In today's world, most people are walking around wearing sunglasses of separateness and seeing only the differences in the world.

Relate this to people. Where is most of a person, where you can see or where you can't see? Suppose most of a human being, much like an island, is where you can't see. What if it is in this unseen realm where you and I are connected just like the islands under the water? Suppose you have an umbilical cord with your boss only, you just can't see it? I suggest that you do. Suppose you have an umbilical cord with your worst enemy? I suggest you do and you just can't see it. If you were connected to everyone, would it make any sense to put yourself down or be intimidated about approaching someone much wealthier than yourself? No it wouldn't. Nor could you put someone else down, because it would be merely a way of putting yourself down.

This way of seeing the world is why the adage of GIVERS GAIN TAKERS LOSE is valid. What you put out you get back. What you sow, so shall you reap. Whatever you do to the least of my brethren you do to me. On the street it was said, what goes around comes around. If one island takes from the other, which one loses? They both do. If one island gives to the other which one gains? They both do. If I can pretend I am a separate island then I can do what I want to you. I can do violence, or live in smugness at my own accumulation of wealth, or live in a world of indifference. Once I get, at a heart level, a number two level (Ch.5) how we are connected, I must act accordingly. To act out of separateness would be suicide.

What do you use to pretend you are separate? Get honest with yourself. Do people have to agree with you, or dress like you, or have the same skin color, or live in the same town to feel connected? Perhaps they must have the same set of values, religious beliefs or economic status? Suppose that it is only a pretense that you are separate while the reality is that you are connected. You just don't see it.

Are the glasses of separateness separating just people? I believe the current pollution of the world is a result of people who have been so caught up in this idea of separateness they think they are separate from the Earth. Simply because human bodies and dirt don't look alike doesn't mean they are separate. One being alive and the other inert are merely two names that describe the small difference observed above the water line. Some of the American Indian language refers to my brother the fox or my brother the bear, etc. There was a connectedness in how they spoke and saw the world.

If China, with one fifth of the world's population,

pollutes in their rush to get the same materialistic benefits the United States average citizen has, do you honestly think you will still be separate? Everyday science is showing more and more the inner-connection between plants, animals, people, and the Earth! There is even a theory—unproven, called GAIA which views the whole Earth as one organism. Are your actions today for the benefit of all or simply for the benefit of some niche at the expense of others? It is the mission of Klemmer and Associates to create, "A World that works for everyone with no one left out". Join the effort. Become a giving maniac. A fanatic about giving and finding win-win solutions.

Giving and win-win are part of a maximum gain philosophy. It is very risky philosophy, but it has the potential for the highest gain. While a separateness philosophy, which is win-lose, initially appears safer, it invariably results in a lower return or even a lose-lose outcome. Let's take a look at this philosophy in a business situation. Remember a time when you saw four gas stations on each corner of an intersection?

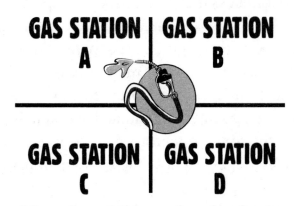

GAS STATION | GAS STATION
A   **B**

GAS STATION | GAS STATION
C   **D**

(We could use four airlines or four fast food restaurants

or four retail stores in this example.) Have you ever seen where gas station A cuts its price by a penny a gallon? Then gas stations B and C also cut their price a penny. Then gas station D cuts it by two pennies. Now gas station A cuts it by 4 pennies. They call this a gas war or price war. It is especially prevalent in recessionary times. Most people think this is "competition". I suggest it is not. It is suicide.

A couple of the gas stations will eventually go out of business. The two left in business then raise their price to try and recover some of what they have lost. It is a lose-lose game. Even the customer is losing because although they get a better initial price the quality of the product goes down, service is reduced, or the safety record suffers.

Now suppose gas station D tries a different stategy. They do not cut their price. All they think about is giving, increasing their service, adding value. If you were to go into gas station D, before your car rolls to a stop someone is rolling underneath your car on a dolly checking if anything needs fixing. Someone else is checking the tire air pressure and cleaning the tires. Someone is washing the windshield and putting in gas. All this and you were just looking for an address?! (All right I am exaggerating a little!)

Now the attendant greets you with a smile, as another way to give to you, and tells you that a few things have been noted that need fixing. "The ones marked in blue we would appreciate you letting us take care of. We have a great price and service for them. The ones we have marked in red we recommend you go to other companies to get taken care of and if you flip the bill over we recommend what companies to go to." Would you go back to this gas station? Of course you would. Why? Because they are doing whatever it takes for you to win, even if it means sending you somewhere else.

A pretty abnormal way of being isn't it? The movie, *Miracle on 34th Street* is the same principle. Now, wouldn't you tell all your friends about gas station D? Of course you would, because you want your friends to win. Now remember, the price you are paying is higher than all the other gas stations, because they cut their price and gas station D did not. Soon all of you reading this and all your friends are going to gas station D. How is gas station D making out financially? They are making a bundle. You win and the customer wins, and the gas station is winning but it doesn't stop there.

The owner of gas station C can see that the owner of gas station D is making a lot of money while everyone else is losing money. So they ask the owner of the gas station out and ask if they would tell the owner of gas station C the secret. If gas station D owner were thinking of separateness they would not tell their competitor the secret. It is what I call the *middle management syndrome* yet it happens at all levels of management It is the thinking that says I won't tell you what I know because if I do I will be out of a job (or prospects, or investment opportunities- you fill in the blank). That is the separateness thinking.

The owner of gas station D in our story is into giving because they see how we are all connected. They go to lunch and the owner of gas station D tells the secret—you need to give more. Be of more service. The owner of gas station D even pays for the lunch of the owner of gas station C as yet another way to give.

Now when gas station owner C increases their giving and being of service, does gas station D lose customers? No. It will seem to some of you that of course they will lose customers, but in the real world they actually gain customers. Why? Because the game of service is infinite, unlike the game of price which is fixed. You can only cut price so much and you are giving it away. Service, however, is infinite.

I could give every reader of this book a block of steel and they could be of service with it in a different way. One could make paper clips, another surgeon scalpels, another a beautiful sculpture. This is the game you want to be competitive in - the game of service. Some of the service that gas station C provides would be the same as gas station D such as smiling attendants but because service is infinite some of the service would be different. Perhaps gas station C would do transmissions and gas station D would do brakes. They have now increased the number of total customers and would actually be sending customers back and forth.

Some of the Klemmer & Associates corporate clients that are made up of sales forces have benefited enormously from this message. Mortgage brokers and real estate agents would cut their commission percentage thinking they would gain volume. Most times they ended up working harder and making less money. Once they kept their prices high and became giving maniacs they made a lot of money.

Now this practice of giving requires knowing what is of service to the customer not merely giving what you want to give or what is traditionally given in the industry. It is extraordinary service. Can you imagine a boss sitting around brainstorming how the employees could make more money? That would be of service. Can you imagine the employees looking for ways to make it easier on the boss? I'm not talking about making decisions that would show the boss up. I am talking about ways that would solve the boss's problems so the boss would work fewer hours! In the competitive workplace I'd take the company thinking this way over the average company every day of the week. In the average company, management pays the employees just enough to keep them from quitting and the employees work just hard enough to keep from getting fired.

This subconcious way of thinking or set of sunglasses comes not just from seeing our bodies as separate.

At the dinner table, at dessert time, the cake was being cut and what went on in your mind? If you had brothers and sisters, I bet I can tell you. You wanted the biggest piece or at least you wanted your fair share. With every piece of cake given away there was less cake. It is what is known in theory as a fixed "pie" game.

Our brain then believes "Oh that's how life is." We start treating everything that way. Some games like price are fixed, but many like service, or love are infinite. Many people who do not have much love in their life are unwilling to give what they have away for fear they will then have nothing left. Once they start giving love they realize even more opens up to them and that it is an infinite game.

The only way this fundamental subconcious thinking or any other paradigm changes can occur is through emotional involvement and repetition. Intellectually knowing about connectedness is not enough. You can know about something and not know it. You can know about a romantic kiss and yet not know it. This is why at Klemmer and Associates we do workshops such as **Personal Mastery, Advanced Leadership, and Heart of the Samurai.** Individuals have experiences where they literally begin to see the world, themselves, and concepts such as commitment, loyalty, responsibility, and giving in a new way. It assists individuals and collectively, corporations, in actually re-evaluating and shifting their fundamental subconcious thinking or sunglasses around reality. Rarely does fundamental thinking or our sunglasses change from books and tapes. The books and tapes provide repetition, but not emotional involvement. The best vehicle of change is a combination of the two.

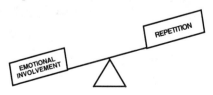

The more emotion involved the less repetition is needed to create lasting change in our subconcious thinking. This is a major key, remember it. Translated, this means the fastest change is possible when you are very emotionally involved. Have you ever heard it takes 21 days to break a habit? I think someone made that up and a lot of people repeat it. In my experience it is not true. I have some habits I changed as fast as you can snap your fingers and other habits I have spent years trying to change and yet they are still not changed. As I look at the difference it seems the amount of emotion involved in making the change was the key difference.

Have you ever known anyone who does not exercise and wants to change that habit or paradigm? Have you noticed it takes months and months before it becomes a habit. The reason it takes much longer than 21 days is that not that much emotion is involved. This is why health clubs have a terrible time keeping clients. They try all kinds of financial gimmicks to try and keep you involved because they know it will take longer than 21 days and by the time that rolls around you will quit.

Now consider someone who has had a heart attack. That is usually pretty emotional. It usually does not take as many heart attacks before someone changes their habits. However, I have been in a hospital and perhaps you have too, where someone who has had a heart attack or stroke is putting fatty food in their mouth or smoking a cigarette. This is a major clue about how strong their subconcious thinking is.

Unless you are very committed, you will get beat by your programs or your subconcious thinking. It is you versus your programs and many of your programs you have lived with for 10- 20 - 30 years (that's a lot of repetition and emotional involvement). Up your commitment to change, NOW.

"Every day man crucifies himself between two thieves

—

the regret of yesterday and the fear of tomorrow"

BENJAMIN DESRAELI

Chapter Nine
An Action Attitude
First Day Last Day

The Question: Do you regret more what you have done, or what you haven't done?

Once upon a time there was a man and a little traveler. (I imagine the little traveler to be wearing leiderhosen and hiking boots.) The man's dream was on top of a great mountain. The man began to sprint up the mountain towards his dream, but you know how mountains go. They get steeper and steeper. Pretty soon our man was not running, he was walking. He soon stopped walking and began to crawl up towards the top of the mountain. It is obvious that the man was very committed. Finally, the man could not go another step and he collapsed on the side of the road.

Along came our little traveler humming and singing. He asked the man what he was doing. The man said he was climbing to the top of the mountain. The little traveler replied, "No you are not, you are resting." "Well, of course I am," said the adult, "climbing to the top of the mountain is hard work." The little traveler then asked the man, "If you want to go to the top of the mountain, why are you wearing that 50-pound sack of manure on your back?" The man was shocked. "There is no sack of manure on my back," he replied. But, sure enough, when he felt his back, he discovered a very heavy 50-pound sack. "Well, I never knew that was there!" he said with surprise. The little traveler asked him if he wanted to keep it. "Of course not," the man answered. "Well then, throw it off the mountain," said the little traveler. The man did and instantly he felt revitalized and refreshed. With renewed vigor, the man sprinted up the side of the mountain, leaving the little traveler in a cloud of dust.

But you know how mountains are. Just like life, they tend to get steeper and tougher and pretty soon our man was walking along huffing and puffing as he went. Soon he began to crawl. He was very committed. Yet he finally collapsed with exhaustion. And do you know who came humming and singing along? The little traveler.

"What are you doing?" he asked the man. Our man replied that he was still trying to climb the mountain, but just had to take a moments rest. The little traveler asked him why in the world he was balancing a 50-pound pumpkin on his head, if what he was trying to do was climb the mountain. The adult said, "That's ridiculous. There is no pumpkin on my head!" But when he checked, to his embarrassment, there was a huge 50-pound pumpkin there. The man started to examine it and reflect on how long it had been there. Maybe it had been there his whole life? The little traveler got frustrated. "Do you want to keep it?" "Of course not! "he replied. "Then get rid of it NOW!" The man threw the huge pumpkin off the mountain.

At the very moment the man chose to move on without the pumpkin was the moment he reached the top of his mountain and his dream. How many sacks of regret and pumpkins of fear are you carrying with you as you climb your mountains and create your dreams?

Knowledge alone is not power; however, applied knowledge is. If you look at the Klemmer & Associates logo it is based around a K + A. That not only stands for Klemmer & Associates, it stands for Knowledge into Action. So many times the twin thieves of fear and regret paralyze us into a state of inaction. An antidote for these twin thieves is the concept of choosing to live as though:

"Today is the first and the last day of the rest of my life."

This idea is a vaccine for the disease of inaction that moves us into an excited state of action.

Let's take the first part, "Today is the first day of the rest of my life." If today was our first day, we wouldn't have any regrets, would we? No, because there would not have been any time to accumulate regrets. Do you remember your first day at work? It was likely filled with an exciting attitude. No matter what the job, your attitude was one of excitement. "Hey - lay it on me. Let me prove to you how much I can do!" A first day attitude is EXCITING.

What happened after you had worked at the job for a few months or years? Perhaps you felt as though the boss played office politics, rewarded others for work you did, didn't pay you what you were worth. Perhaps you stopped showing up early and excited. Maybe you began to show up for work just on time and didn't have the passion you once had.

Tomorrow, after reading this, play what may seem a silly game and go to work as though it was your first day again. Choose to look at your job through sunglasses of the day being your first day and just see what happens!

Try it as an experiment. Can you remember the attitude you approached your first date with? It was exciting! Nervous maybe, but it was exciting. That is a first day attitude. But, what happened after you had been in relationship with that person for years? Perhaps you accumulated regrets on your back when you forgot an anniversary card, or said or did something unwise, or you let an opportunity to communicate pass you by, and pretty soon you were carrying a few pounds of rocks on your back and you weren't so excited in the relationship anymore.

Well, today if you are in a romantic relationship, pretend you are meeting them for the first time. If that means you would dress up or buy them flowers, then do that! Forget whether you think they deserve it, that thinking is based on the past. Simply choose to look at the realtionship through a set of sunglasses called "today is your first day." In my experience most marriages which end in divorce do not do so because of one big blow out. They end as a result of a slow leak caused by resentments and regrets that each person begins to carry on their back and that slows their climb up the mountain of marriage.

Do you remember the first time one of your children rolled over? If you have children, of course you do! "Honey, she rolled over! She's going to be an Olympic gymnast. Did you see the form?!!" But, what happened when they had rolled over 1,000 times? You weren't as excited anymore. And after they messed up your new carpet? And after they started back talking you or goofing off in school? Maybe you lost that first day attitude and you started saying things like, "Would you just let me read the paper?" Well, today, even if your children are grown, pretend it's your first day with them. Pretend you have never met them before and just see what happens.

What a relief a first day attitude is. No grudges. No regrets of a childhood that wasn't the way we wanted. No regrets of relationships that didn't work out or ones we let slip by from not acting on them. No regrets of bad decisions or foolish actions. This first day outlook is exciting!

When Disney comes out with a movie like *The Little Mermaid*, I am always astounded by our daughters ability to watch it one hundred times. She has a first day attitude each time she sees it and so it is exciting. Cultivate this attitude and you will add an excitement about life that others only dream about.

The second part, "Today is the last day of the rest of your life," is a call to action. It is an attitude of urgency. Not panic, but a "do it now" attitude. If you only had 24 hours to live on this planet as we know it, you would not be putting things off until tomorrow simply because there wouldn't be a tomorrow. If you somehow knew you had only 24 hours to live and you arrived home and your spouse was upset, do you think you would get upset or allow them to stay that way? Not a chance! You might say to them, "we don't have time for this. Let's do something that matters. Let's talk about the kids and what's important to us." Do that NOW!

Instead of watching TV or waiting for the "right time" or when it's comfortable or convenient, DO IT NOW! Put down the book now and communicate something important to someone you love or care for. This is a last day attitude.

If you only had 24 hours to live and you have children then you would do what ever they asked you to. You would not say, "I'll do it next week" would you? Of course not. You would take them to the park if they wanted, even if it was dark. Do that now. That's the urgency of a last day attitude.

Do you know when most people get a last day attitude? When they perceive it to really be their last day. Someone gets seriously ill and they start acting with urgency about their health. Until then, there is no urgency, no last day attitude. There is an attitude that says "there is plenty of time and it won't happen to me." It's so easy if you have young children to believe you have plenty of time with them. I'll work hard now and catch up with them later. But, do you know you have plenty of time? No, not for sure you don't.

The guarantee we will live until age 75 is an illusion.

I think this attitude of inaction occurs because so much is guaranteed to most of us living in first world countries. Most of you reading this book would not buy a car, stereo, or appliance without some guarantee. Sometimes in seminars, I have people pull out their wallets and purses and count up the guarantees they carry with them. They are astounded. Credit cards guarantee we can buy things. ATM cards guarantee we can get money out of the bank without special hours. Pictures guarantee memories. Life insurance guarantees our heirs will be provided for. Medical insurance guarantees we will be medically cared for when sick. Library cards and drivers licenses are guarantees.

These are not bad guarantees. They give us more liberty. The problem, in part, is that we assume life is also guaranteed until we are 75. You don't think so? Have you ever been in an argument, and said to yourself, "I don't want to handle this now, I'll handle it later?" You were not living from a view point of today is the last day of my life.

You might be saying to yourself—"Well, if today was the last day, I would do things different. I wouldn't go to work." Then maybe you are in the wrong job! If the only reason you are going to work is to collect a paycheck, you are blowing it. You are trading your life for a very small price. If your life was about making a difference, you would spend part of your last day at work, because there are opportunities there to make a difference. If your work is a vehicle for the expression of yourself, you would spend a part of your last day at work.

There are plenty of jobs for you to make all the money you want. TRUTH. Find something that is a vehicle to fulfill your purpose. You—your life—are too valuable to trade for anything mediocre. When a person does not go after their dream, everyday a piece of them dies.

Perhaps it's a slow process, so people don't see the price they are paying. Then one day they realize they are walking zombies. They are survivors existing in life, but not living a full life.

Take action today on what matters to you! If today was the last day of your life and you could do any 10 items that you wrote down, what would they be? In other words, if you wanted to travel around the world, even though that takes longer than 24 hours in real time, you could get it done, if you wrote it as one of your ten items. If you wanted to invent the cure for AIIDS— done! Anything you wanted, you could have, do or be. Take this seriously and don't cop out with things like, "write ten more items." Write down 10 items before you go on. Make sure you take this seriously. Write down what matters most to you.

1.

2.

3.

4.

5.

6.

7.

8.

9.

10.

Did you do it? No? Then you don't have a last day attitude. If you have written them great! Now take action on one of the items right now. If you wrote something grandiose like solve world hunger—then look through the telephone book and find an organization that feeds the hungry and call and volunteer some time. I'm not saying solve the whole problem now. I am saying take action NOW! Do not wait until you have enough money, or it's comfortable, or it's convenient, or it feels right. ACT now. That's a last day attitude.

Right now, take action on one of those items. If God grants you another day then take action on another item. Tell someone you love that you love them or attempt to repair a broken relationship. Pick up the phone now and start. Make an attempt!

Chapter Ten Rags to Riches
Applying the Philosophy

The Question: How big are you daring to dream?

 **There** are many people we could study in this chapter. Of the thousands who have done our workshops in companies, public seminars and within network marketing companies there are many people who have produced tangible incredible results. Marriages have been saved, weight loss has been achieved, people have stopped smoking, changed to jobs that were satisfying, incomes have been significantly increased, and many different dreams achieved.

I wanted to write in depth about someone who went from nothing to something of significance, simply by applying the philosophy, in order to give people hope. This person could be a beacon of possibilities for people. If at some point in the future beyond my writting of this book, fortunes take a turn for the worse, he will still be a beacon of hope because he will recreate it. That's part of his secret. Alan is not afraid to lose. I want people to say that if Alan can do it, I certainly can do it.

One of my mentor's main messages to me was "I (meaning my mentor) am nobody special. Whatever I have done, anybody can do—if they are willing to pay the prices and apply the philosophy". The following facts and summary are not intended to promote this person as someone special, but as a message of hope as to what is possible when an ordinary person applies the philosophy. The person I chose to be this beacon of hope is Alan Nagao. He is awarded the first annual Product of the Philosophy Award. Alan was a student in a seminar I was facilitating in 1988. At the time he was 24 years old. Alan was born in Hawaii and went to high school. He was not a standout academically and he chose not to go to college. He was not the most popular child and not particularly athletic. In fact, he was born without a leg and has a deformed hand. Many people who meet him today aren't even aware at first of his physical differences because he has no energy on that aspect of himself.

At the age of 20 Alan started his own company, High Performance Kites. When I first met Alan, he was earning about $600 a month selling kites. $60 in one day was a big day for him. Even though this was a few years ago, it still was not very much money. Alan set a goal of owning a store in the major shopping mall in Honolulu called Ala Moana. It was a prestigious site and very difficult to get into. He had no track record or financial history to warrant getting in. He was turned down twice before being approved. (Persistence should be his middle name.) Alan still has his store in the Ala Moana shopping mall.

Alan began expanding and decided to create a yo-yo boom in Hawaii. The state of Hawaii only has 1 million people. Yo-Yo's obviously are not a necessity for people and at the time were not very popular. Using the visualization techniques discussed in this book he created a marketing plan around how to create a yo-yo need. Alan created such a yo-yo boom in Hawaii he outsold the rest of the whole United States. He then looked at Japan.

This is a true Formula of Champions story we spoke of in Chapter 2. Alan had no contacts in Japan nor did he speak the language. The much needed manufacturer of yo-yo's was not returning his phone calls or faxes. He was almost out of financing and his wife Priscilla, unknown to Alan, had pulled money out of their life insurance policy to finance the last trip to the manufacturer. Undeterred, Alan set a goal of selling 1 million yo-yo's in Japan. Alan ended up selling over 10 million yo-yo's in Japan. This was the largest single yo-yo boom in the world ever.

In 1998 along with a very good friend, Lance Giroux, we did HPK's corporate conference as they grossed approximately $13 million. This is substantial growth from $600/month income to grossing approximately $13 million a year. What parts of the philosophy did Alan apply that you can too? That very question was the reason and subject matter for an interview I did with Alan in 1999 that is now a part of our *Mastery of Money* tape series. Not all of Alan's attention or success, however, was in business. Along the way, Alan married Priscilla and they now have two beautiful children. They have a great relationship and are wonderful people.

During Alan's development of HPK Marketing

he took 7 months off to deepen his relationship with his own father by building a house. Alan and Priscilla are also active in the community and in humanitarian organizations such as the YMCA. As president of the YMCA of Hawaii, Alan volunteers his time believing that as we give, so shall we receive. Alan is an example of the balance we discussed in Chapter 7.

How many people do you know who are so busy chasing their own success they complain of not having enough time?! None of this is to say that Alan is perfect and does not make mistakes. He makes mistakes just like anyone else. In fact he plans on it! One of his motto's is that to up your success rate, up your failure rate. He believes that in marketing alone, half of the ideas will fail and so he has created a system for handling the failures. Simple things like test marketing ideas in a small market where he limits the downside of his failure and leverages his successes are part of that system.

There are graduates of the seminars who have created larger companies, so this is not to say Alan and Priscilla are the only stars. They started with nothing, have created a balanced life of financial success, family life, belief in God, and contribution to others. If they can do it – so can you. In fact, why not? I can't think of any good reason, can you?

The Lesson   I asked Alan what aspects of the philosophy he applied the most. Here are 10 key points I picked up on as we did the interview. #1—He is a fanatic on vision and goals. He has a written goal statement that is on his desk, in his car, and he says it out loud several times a day. #2—Alan spends time to learn. He took 3 years to learn, apply, and perfect the visualization technique from the seminar. Most people do it once or twice and think they understand it. Perhaps his secret was that because he would fall asleep in the beginning, he figured he needed to work on the technique. He went to other seminars, hired a success tutor, read, and practiced visualization daily. Are you willing to invest time in really digesting the material in this book? #3—He is persistent. Whether it's continuing to send faxes to a manufacturer after they asked him not to or repeatedly asking for space in Ala Moana shopping mall after being turned down, he focuses on what he wants and continues to take action. #4—He plays life for maximum gain whereas most people play life not to lose. He could have rested on his success in Hawaii, but he risked by taking on Japan. He could have rested again after the success in Japan but he took on 6 new countries and expanded from 7 employees to over 60. Alan is willing to risk for the potential maximum gain. #5—He recognizes that we are creatures of habit. In his business he sets up systems to insure successful habits for giving, for risking, for handling failure, for communication, for learning. In his personal life he has systems such as daily use of the visualization technique. #6—He believes in God. He purposely takes on challenges he knows he cannot do as a way of forcing his subconscious and God to come to his aid. #7—He works on the principle of balance. He spends time working on his relationships, health, spirituality, and work in the community. #8—He practices the principle of giving and contribution to others. In 1998 he gave away $120,000 personally. This was possible because he was willing to struggle and give away $60 when he only made $600 a month. Alan provides his employees with company-paid time for them to give to the community. *#9*—He practices visualization as a way to creatively solve problems. Whether it is developing a way to create a boom for yo-yo's or making a decision as to what opportunity to pursue next, he utilizes visualization to go beyond what reason and logic alone can solve. #10- He believes in the team and a win-win approach. Whether it is two employees or his company HPK and a manufacturer, he truly wants to see everyone both work together and benefit together.

Many people of my generation, the baby boomers, have spent too much energy and time trying to find themselves. Let this story be the end of trying to discover yourself. Instead, let it be the beginning of creating your life story. Dare to dream your impossible dream. What would you do if you knew you couldn't fail? Have the courage to go after it. Have the discipline to apply the philosophy on a daily basis. You can do it.

Epilogue

Mastery is the ability to create the experience we want, regardless of the circumstances presented. Most people believe that they can be successful only if the circumstances are right. Rarely in either business or one's personal life do all the circumstances line up as we want or expect.

Mastery has very little to do with intelligence. You probably know some highly-educated people who are unemployed or who are in failed relationships. Mastery is the ability to create what you want. Now if you want financial independence, you create it and you create it quickly—that's the Mastery. The difference between a master and an aprentice or novice is the amount of time it takes to create. A master quickly creates, and a novice takes awhile.

This book is about you being a Master of Life. Mastery gives you liberty—the ability to do what you want to do, when you want to do it, not just when someone with authority says you can or can't. It is the ability to go where you want to go when you want to go there, not just when someone says you can go there. Most importantly it is the ability to be what you want to be when you want to be that way.

Mastery is proactive—it's not a destination. Think of someone in sports—business—art—relationships, who you consider to be a Master. They are into the practice, not just the end result. At the time of the writing of this book, Jerry Rice is a football player. He is one of, if not, the greatest receivers ever in the game. He has set numerous records - total yards gained, number of catches in the game, to name a few. He is the first player on the field and the last off from practice. He practices the art of receiving. It is a practice, not just the end result. An artist or musician who is a Master, is into the practice. It is a regular daily thing, not just a paid performance.

Mastery is a combination of awareness and skills. Being a Master would be the consistent application of this philosophy and the ability to apply it and get results.

I have a belief and it may not be true. The sunglasses I have chosen to look through, is that it is God's plan for you to prosper in all areas of your life. If you are not prospering in all areas, it is not His fault. It is simply you have not mastered the game of life and how to play it *the way it was designed to be played.* If you are Christian, as I am, the Bible says in 3 John 1:2 "I wish above all things that thou mayest prosper and be in health even as thy soul propereth". To me, that means, in all of our natures, physical, mental, emotional and spiritual we are to experience abundance. If you are of another faith, look through your Holy book. Whatever you choose to call God, he wants to be proud of you. If you have no belief in God, then my prayers are that this book has opened a door for you to explore the possibility of a being greater than yourself or having a higher consciousness, a level 3 as referred in Chapter 5. If you do believe, it is not to say the road will be easy. Masters of the game of life have bigger challenges, but they are prepared. A belief in God is not for the benefit solely of this world. However, it is a huge advantage in playing the game of life.

One of my dear friends is Jay Golby. He has also been my financial planner. He once said, "Open up your checkbook to me, and I will tell you what is important to you." The same can be said of your time. Tell me how much time you spend on what and I will tell you what's important to you. Usually, time and money are very good indicators of the truth. If you do not spend time and money with your family, do not try telling me they are important to you. If you do not spend time and money on God or your 3rd level of being, do not try and tell me He's important to you. If you do not spend time and money on books, tapes, seminars to educate yourself in being a Master - one able to produce or create results- then do not tell me it is important to you.

Are you willing to spend the next 20 years studying the material in this book? If not, you do not want to be a Master. You want to be a walking encyclopedia who can spout the words, sound like you know the game, but really you only know about the game as we talked about it in this book. **The fairest way to gauge anything is by results, often harsh, always fair.**

Begin to live like an eagle. Choose the life of an eagle where you have the liberty to do what you want to do, go where you want to go, and be what you want to be. It may be more dangerous than the life of an oyster as the conditions are not as constant as that of an oyster and there is more rejection. The oyster lives in fairly safe conditions; however, it has little liberty and lives on the leftovers from other animals. The eagle fails 60-70% of the time it goes after its prey, but it always gets its prey because it is persistent and goes back again and again until it gets what it is after. It enjoys the freedom of the skies. It has vision where it can spot a dime, one quarter of a mile away.

Are you going to be an oyster or an eagle? If you are an eagle and are about applying the knowledge of this book, then take the following ACTION PLAN into your life.

Each week take on one idea—one chapter of this book. Every day for one week read the same chapter. Everyday consciously, pro-actively, apply the concept at least once. Plan out ahead of time how to do this. At the end of the week you move on to the next idea and chapter. This will take you approximately 20 minutes a day to do the reading and a few more minutes applying the idea. It will take you about 2 months to get through the book and then, you can start over again.

Can you get muscles watching me lift weights? No, of course not. It does you very little good to be impressed by me. Lift your own weights. If you were going to get your body in shape it would take you more than a half hour a day for 3 months. It would be a practice for life. Your working out is the same game to mentally build the muscles that the chapters in this book discuss.

Now the question is simply - will you? It starts with a commitment. Will you commit - make an agreement-for the next 90-days to follow the plan? If you do and you complete the 90 day workout, send us your name and address and some of your wins along with $2.50 for shipping and handling. We rely on your integrity. We will send you a free tape valued at $10 as our way of saying congratulations in taking your life on in such a huge way.

The Need for Leadership in the United States

1. 1 in 2 live in a single parent family at some point in their childhood
2. 1 in 3 five to seventeen-year-olds are behind a year or more in school
3. 1 in 4 is born to a mother who did not graduate from highschool
4. 1 in 7 have no health insurance
5. 1 in 8 drop out of school
6. 1 in 9 is born into a family living at less than half of the poverty level ($6,490 for family of three)
7. 1 in 12 has a disability
8. 1 in 25 is reported abused or neglected in any given year
9. 1 in 120 die before their 1st birthday
10. 1 in 610 will be killed by a gun before their 20th birthday
11. 1 in 5 lives in a family that receives food stamps
12. 1 in 3 is born to an unmarried parent

The Need for Leadership in the World

1. 50% of the World does not have clean sanitation water
2. 20% of the World does not have shelter
3. 33% of the World goes to bed hungry
4. 3% die of hunger every year
5. 70% of the World is unable to read
6. Only 1% are college educated

It does not have to be this way. The time for you to work on your leadership is now.

Recommended Reading

A Book A Month for One Year

Mastery — George Leonard
Rich Dad, Poor Dad — Robert Kiyosaki
Body for Life — Bill Phillips
Mach 2—With Your Hair on Fire — Richard Brooke
Magic of Conflict — Tom Crumm
Riches Within Your Reach — Robert Collier
Operating Manual for Spaceship Earth
R. Buckminster Fuller
The Business of Discovering the Future
Joel Barker
Think & Grow Rich — Napoleon Hill
100th Monkey — Ken Keyes Jr.
The Game of Life & How to Play It
Florence Scovel Shinn
7 Habits of Highly Effective People — Steven Covey
Sacred Hoops — Phil Jackson
I Dare You — William Danforth
Psychocybernetics — Dr. Maxwell Maltz
Winning Through Enlightenment — Ron Smotherman
Diet for a New America — John Robbins
Bible or your own religious book

The Pursuit & Practice of Personal Mastery

Mastery is a process of integrity through which you can create superior results with ease. If you have ever had a burning desire and still not been able to produce the result you want, this cassette series is for you. If you see that people do not necessarily do what they know is good for themselves nor what they are told ,then you will enjoy exploring how you think life works. In these ten tapes you'll learn unique perspectives to create new levels of success in relationships in your life, results, and with a balanced quality of life. This series is the basis for the best selling book *"If How-To's Were Enough, We Would All be Skinny, Rich, and Happy"*.

$80.00 + $5.00 shipping and handling

Mastery of Money

Are you working harder and yet feel like you are not getting ahead financially? Are you looking to become a master of money versus being its slave? Do you want to know how the really rich think and handle money versus how the middle class do? Learn about the 8 major myths of money and the 6 ways that the rich think about money. Hear how one person applied the concepts and went from $600 a month selling kites to grossing $12 million in a year. Hear from experts such as the best selling author of *Rich Dad, Poor Dad*, Robert Kiyosaki or from the coach to the very wealthy on asset protection, Manny Martinez.

$65.00 + $5.00 shipping and handling

The CASHFLOW® Learning Package

This is the single greatest investment you can make in your financial future. Do you want to be financially independent yet lack financial IQ? Has learning financial fundamentals seemed boring? In this fun, breakthrough learning experience you will learn all the financial fundamentals one needs for financial independence as well as explore your beliefs around money. The learning package includes 3 audio cassettes, and video by Robert Kiyosaki , the author of the best selling book *Rich Dad Poor Dad,* as well as the experiential board game. This is not available in any stores.

$200.00 + $10.00 shipping and handling

Brian Klemmer is an authorized distributor for CASHFLOW®. CASHFLOW® is a registered trademark of CASHFLOW Technologies, Inc.

A Zoo With a View

What could be more important than communicating values to our children? The Zoo Book is for ages 3-10. In 6 delightful animal stories the values of 1) not settling for what we have 2) making a difference for others 3) the importance of vision balanced by learnable steps 4) the benefit of being vulnerable 5) opportunity versus security 6) handling peer pressure. A tape with 20 similar stories for use by adults in sales or management meetings is also available.

——— TO PLACE AN ORDER ———

- Call toll free **1-800-577-5447**
- Fax (415) 899-0278
- Contact us through our website
  www.klemmer.com

Corporate Workshops

- Do your sales need a boost?
- Have you experienced fast growth and communciation is a problem?
- Has a project gotten behind its time line?
- Have you experienced a restructuring that is struggling to meet expectations?
- Have you tried the typical teamwork trainings and are looking for something different that really works?

Klemmer & Associates Inc. is an internationally recognized consulting firm that produces results. Its client list includes well-known companies such as

- Hewlett Packard
- American Suzuki Motor Company
- Los Angeles Federal Credit Union
- ITT Sheraton
- Ricoh Copiers

We also work with smaller hospitals, manufacturing firms, sales forces and boards of directors.

We offer a free test drive with one of our training modules for the decision maker and those corporations with a sincere interest in working with us in the future.

If you are interested in improving the bottom line by training leaders of character for the next century then call 1-800-577-5447 for more information on putting us to work for you!

Keynotes

Brian Klemmer is a sought after keynote speaker who for over twenty years on three different continents, has moved people with thought provoking and humorous speeches. If you are a meeting planner or are responsible for company or association meetings and looking for a memorable, content significant, uplifting speaker contact Blue Feather Management at 888-797-6700 and arrange to have Brian Klemmer at your next function.

Network Marketing Trainings

Duplication is the key to this industry. Typical training is limited to the "how to's" of the business. If you are a top income earner and would like your downline to increase their productivity immediately and for the long term by experientially exploring their understanding of such topics as responsibility and commitment, then call the corporate Klemmer & Associates office at 1-800-577-5447. Single evening and one day programs are available as well as the life changing Personal Mastery weekends. You must be able to put together a 100 distributors minimum for an evening presentation or 50 distributors for the popular result producing weekend seminar.

1. Personal Mastery — A Friday night, Saturday and Sunday seminar based around the content of this book and held in different cities around the world.

2. Advanced Leadership Training — Created to transform your experience of yourself so that you are more effective personally and professionally this 5 day intensive leadership workshop is offered and held only in San Francisco.

3. Children's Personal Mastery — A Saturday Sunday version of the adult seminar done for ages 5-12 through skits, puppets, and games.

4. Teen Leadership Experience — Offered for 13-17 year olds once a year. It is a five-day live-in experience where they explore trust, respect, handling peer pressure, courage, self esteem, leadership, and releasing anger.

5. Heart of the Samurai — A five day, ultimate experience at playing the game of life at the highest level. This is for those wanting to not only create abundance for themselves, but contribute to others in a very significant way.

All current locations and dates are available through our website **www.klemmer.com** or by phone 1-800-577-5447.